THE TRANSPLANTED EXECUTIVE

THE TRANSPLANTED EXECUTIVE

Why You Need to Understand
How Workers in Other Countries
See the World Differently

P. CHRISTOPHER EARLEY
MIRIAM EREZ

New York   Oxford
OXFORD UNIVERSITY PRESS
1997

Oxford University Press

Oxford New York
Athens   Aukland   Bangkok   Bogotá   Bombay
Buenos Aires   Calcutta   Cape Town   Dar es Salaam   Delhi
Florence   Hong Kong   Istambul   Karachi
Kuala Lumpur   Madras   Madrid   Melbourne
Mexico City   Nairobi   Paris   Singapore
Taipei   Tokyo   Toronto

and associated companies in
Berlin   Ibadan

Library of Congress Cataloging-in-Publication Data
Earley, P. Christopher.
The transplanted executive:
why you need to understand how workers in
other countries see the world differently/
P. Christopher Earley, Miriam Erez.
p cm.
Includes bibliographical references and index.
ISBN 0-19-508795-X
1. International business enterprises—Management.
2. International business enterprises—Personnel management.
3. Employee motivation. 4. Intercultural communication.
I. Erez, Miriam. II. Title.
HD62.4.E24   1997   658'.049—dc20   96-9286

1 3 5 7 9 8 6 4 2

Printed in the United States of America
on acid-free paper

PREFACE

In this age of the globalization of business, managers frequently find themselves transplanted to a new work setting. This is a book for managers who may be moving to a work culture that is different from the one they know. This could be to another part of their home country that may have a different work culture, or to another country altogether. There is a very good chance that workers there will not be receptive to the management practices that have been effective with your present workers. The results could be disastrous.

It is natural that, as a manager, you use your experience on the job and your own value system to work effectively with your superiors, peers, and subordinates. However, when you move to a new situation where the workers are in a different culture, and do not share your experiences at work or your value system, they may not respond as you expect. You may not be able to understand them and to get their commitment to the assignment you have been given.

In this book we provide the tools for understanding workers in different kinds of cultures so that you can adjust your management practices accordingly. The key to success begins with understanding yourself and your culture. We therefore include a tool for assessing yourself and your cultural values, what we call self-knowledge. We tell you how to interpret the measure and how to use it in assessing the self-knowledge and cultural values of your new employees. We divide cultures into four types based on self-knowledge and cultural values, and we show which countries fall into each type. We have created a number of tables that allow you to look up the country to which you are moving to determine what kinds of workers you will find there and learn what managerial and motivational practices will be most effective with them. We also provide explicit guidance on communicating, motivating, forming teams, leadership, and quality, in different cultures.

Our decision to write this book stems from our work with business executives who work in international settings. Time after time, we have been approached by expatriate managers who have encountered management problems that result from cultural misunderstandings. We hope that you can find the book a useful guide for handling the complexities of management in the globalized world of business.

September 1996   P. C. E.
                                                             M. E.

ACKNOWLEDGEMENTS

There are many people who helped shape this book including our universities, colleagues, students, and our families. First, we would like to thank our universities—the University of California at Irvine, School of Management, and Technion-Israel Institute of Technology—for their continuing support of our international work.

In addition, we want to acknowledge the valuable input that was provided by faculty at various universities including: The London Business School, Nanyang Technological University (Singapore), University of South Carolina, and Hong Kong University of Science and Technology. The second author wants to thank her colleagues, and students around the world. In particular, she would like to thank Tamao Matsui from Surugadai University in Japan, ed Locke and Ben Schneider from the University of Illinois, Sheldon Zedeck from the University of California at Berkeley, Terry Mitchell from Washington University, and Michael Bond and Kowk Leung, from the Chinese University of Hong Kong. Jane George-Falvi and Linda Mattheus were most helpful in editing some of the book chapters.

We would like to thank the staff at Oxford for their editorial guidance (and patience), and we would especially like to thank Herb Addison for his guidance and suggestions concerning the shaping of our earlier drafts of this book.

Finally, and most important, we want to thank our families. The first author thanks Jiminy, Sport, and Whidbey for helping Elaine keep her sanity during his various trips to Israel in writing this book. The second author would like to thank her husband Lipa, her daughter Mor, and her son Mattan, for their valuable love, support, and sharing.

CONTENTS

THE TRANSPLANTED EXECUTIVE

1

Introduction: Managing the Global Enterprise

A seemingly simple question has led us to examine the management practices of numerous successful companies for their key to success: why are many managerial and motivational techniques useful in one country but often not in others? Numerous examples bring home this basic dilemma facing the modern manager. For example, quality control circles resoundingly successful in Japanese companies, have proved to be only somewhat effective when implemented in U.S. companies. One-on-one performance appraisals, though widely used throughout the United States, are rarely employed in other countries; when they are used, they often create more management confusion than success. Individual job-enrichment programs like job rotation, job enlargement, and empowerment have been the focus of managerial change in the United States but have taken a very different form in the Scandinavian countries. The focus of enrichment in the United States places responsibility on the individual, whereas enrichment in socialist countries such as Sweden concentrates on the work team. The individual motivation underlying pay-for-performance reward systems, emphasized in companies such as Xerox Corporation, General Motors, and Intel Corporation in the United States, are unacceptable in group and team-oriented cultures such as those found in central European nations like the Czech Republic and Hungary, where more egalitarian approaches are used.[1]

To complicate matters further, managers often find that several of the very same techniques may work in one country for a limited time only to run into problems later. For example, General Motors had a number of early and dramatic successes with its Saturn division. Most of General Motors's automobile and truck divisions,such as Chevrolet and Cadillac, have approached car manufacturing using traditional assembly lines, union-management division, and variable quality output. By contrast the Saturn division quickly entered the market as a "new horizon."[2] How could such a highly centralized and traditional company produce the progressive Saturn division and successfully implement management techniques foreign to General Motors, such as salaries for production workers and staff alike as well as team-based production, employee quality control, and empowerment? Saturn's manufacturing plant was based on ideas of autonomous work team, employee empowerment and responsibility, and extensive training and development. The result of these innovative management practices was success and media attention. The Saturn car was viewed as superior to other American cars and on a par with Japanese and German competition.

Yet despite its successes, the Saturn division recently has faced a number of problems. First, suspicion and resentment from other General Motors divisions, which view it as an "overindulged child," detract from its own marketing and production efforts. This suspicion has led former chairman Robert Stempel to question the need for further investment in the Saturn division and the general corporate office to mandate central control of marketing and advertising for the division. Second, there have been increasing concerns over productivity within the plant, employee uneasiness about the management practices, labor problems, and so forth. Can the successes of the young Saturn plant overcome these more recent limitations and challenges? Can this style of management innovation work in other General Motors plants, each with their own cultures, in the United States? Why hasn't General Motors already shifted over its management approach to the Saturn team style? Will the auto workers from the Midwest respond to empowerment and teamwork as strongly as workers from the South? The Northwest? Should General Motors export its successful Saturn experiences to its assembly plants in Europe?

Unfortunately, present approaches to management do not provide answers either to these questions or to the issue of why managing people takes such diverse forms in the workplace as companies move across international borders. The response that we suggest here is fundamental: the key to managing diverse people is knowing yourself and understanding them.

A New Way of Thinking About You, Your Values, and Culture in a Global Workplace

The main purpose of our book is to help managers work more effectively in a multicultural workplace. This cultural diversity may be global or simply regional. Our approach to managerial effectiveness incorporates a manager's personal values and needs, cultural values, and managerial practices. The effectiveness of motivational techniques and managerial practices depend to a large extent on their perceived usefulness and contribution toward achieving personal and organizational goals. The usefulness is judged according to norms and values that vary from one country or region to another. From the perspective of an employee, the value of managerial techniques is determined according to opportunities afforded that individual for developing his or her potential and for satisfying personal needs. From a company's perspective, the usefulness of applying certain managerial techniques depends on the extent to which the techniques harness human resources to achieve corporate objectives. The following is an example of the cultural dilemma that we are discussing.

CTX

CTX is a highly successful high-technology company based in Israel.[3] Its main product is highly sophisticated equipment used in the printing industry. Within a few years, CTX has grown into a multinational company with a total of sixteen subsidiaries in Europe, the United States, and Japan. The main purpose of the subsidiaries is to provide service and maintenance of the printing machines produced in Israel.

Corporate headquarters was faced with serious communication problems with its subsidiaries. Managers in the subsidiaries were not providing the required reports on daily activities or special problems with maintenance and service; such feedback was essential for the head office to monitor the subsidiaries and to learn about the special needs of foreign customers. The general manager decided to invite the managers of all the subsidiaries to Israel and have them participate in a workshop designed to improve communication. The workshop was designed as a role play during which the headquarters' staff emphasized the importance of communication and allowed the subsidiary managers to explain why they did not submit the anticipated communiqués. Managers from the subsidiaries and the headquarters were divided into two groups, one representing the subsidiaries, the other representing the head office. Each group was asked to prepare reasons for its actions for the meeting with the other group. Next the two groups got together in an attempt to find the reasons that underlay the problem.

The Israeli headquarters representative started the meeting by saying; "First of all, you are all fired, and second, you have two minutes to explain why you did not respond to our questions." The manager of the Italian subsidiary said with emotion, "Vendetta" (meaning revenge) and "You, the headquarters, used to ask me to send you reports and data on customers and services, but you never told me what you did with it. You have not provided any feedback or comparative data on other subsidiaries. Therefore I refuse to provide any additional information."

The Belgian manager politely said, "No response is also a response." What he meant was that if he did not respond, there was a reason for it. What he expected from home office was for it to pay attention and find out what was bothering him. The Israeli manager was not used to the subtle style of the Belgian nor the antagonistic style of the Italian. He could not understand how no response constituted a reply. He raised his voice and angrily stated that subsidiaries should be loyal to the head office and no subsidiary should dare to refuse to communicate any requested information.

Clearly this mutual misunderstanding illustrates a potential problem arising from cultural diversity, and the importance of culture in understanding the effectiveness of management practices. The Israeli managers from CTX had a direct, authoritative style, acquired during their mandatory military service (young Israeli males provide three years of mandatory military service; two years for women after they complete high school followed by short-term, yearly duty until their mid-fifties). At the same time, Israeli culture is known for its emphasis on equality and work participation. Thus Israeli employees are not threatened by an authoritarian style because they interpret it as assertiveness and decisiveness rather than manipulation and domination.

Though the dominant managerial values in many European countries also emphasize workplace democracy and participation, the European managers in this case were offended by the direct and authoritarian approach of the Israelis. They interpreted this as an attempt to use brute power, manipulation, and control and reacted to the Israeli managerial style as a personal threat and intimidation. As a result, they protected their egos either by acting in kind, by having thoughts of revenge (in the case of the Italian manager), or by avoiding or denying (in the case of the Belgian manager). The Europeans felt resentment rather than loyalty and cooperation with the Israeli headquarters. Their cultural values were similar but not identical to the Israelis.

Motorola

The CTX dilemma is repeated more times than many managers would like to admit. For instance, we spoke with a key human resources manager (HRM) from Motorola who is responsible for staffing efforts in the Pacific Rim. He described a new venture that Motorola had started in mainland China that uses the company's emphasis on total quality management, or what it refers to as six-sigma quality (we will discuss the quality improvement approach more in Chapter 8). A key aspect of this approach is that every employee takes on the responsibility of quality control and work initiative. The HRM manager commented that one of his biggest challenges was to recruit Chinese employees willing to assume the individual responsibility needed for Quality Improvement (QI). As in many Asian countries, Chinese workers are expected to conform and not show a great deal of individual initiative and independent action such as questioning someone else's work. After a number of false starts attempting to "empower" the typical Chinese worker, Motorola now takes a very different approach.[4] During a very early orientation, Motorola tells prospective employees exactly what is expected of them; if they are not comfortable with these expectations, they are asked to quit the program. Rather than refocus the QI technique, Motorola is relying on a large labor pool in China that will provide enough "good fits" for the company. What is interesting about the Motorola case is that trying to change people's basic values, the company selected an approach in which it lets people "select" themselves according to their personal needs. This situation, in which people are fit into the existing company, illustrates an important point about self-knowledge and cultural values: not everyone in a single culture can be expected to react similarly to a given managerial technique.

In the example of CTX, the emphasis was on exporting a particular management style and ignoring the specific values of subsidiary managers. In the case of Motorola, the general method of QI has not been adapted to the specific cultural values found in the workers of mainland China. In neither case did the companies use an integrated approach to managing employees' varying cultural values. It is this integrated approach of cultural values and self-knowledge that is the foundation of our book.

The Organization of the Book

This book is divided into two parts. The first consists of two chapters that explain our approach and how to apply it generally. Chapter 2 discusses the concepts that underlay our approach and includes a self-scoring diagnostic tool that you can use to determine personal and cultural values of both you and your employees. Chapter 3 describes how to apply the concepts in a general managerial situation using employee motivation as an example. In the second part of the book, we apply our approach to a number of important managerial topics, including effective communication, motivation, teamwork, leadership, and quality management production. Finally, Chapter 9 summarizes our approach and provides some final conclusions and recommendations for becoming an effective global manager.

How to Use This Book

More than any other purpose, we have designed this book to be a resource for a manager who is on the verge of an overseas assignment, is making a regional move within his or her country, or is confronted with a diverse new work team. In order to make the most of the book, we have provided a series of quick reference tables and charts at the end of each chapter. We organized these tables using our framework, and we have offered a number of specific examples in each one. To begin, you should look to Table 2.1 for a general table of countries and profiles. Although this listing is not comprehensive, we have provided the profiles of nearly fifty countries from major business centers in Europe, Asia, North and South America, the Middle East, and Africa. Once you have determined the general profile for the country in which you are interested, you can use this profile and cross-reference it with the charts listed at the end of each chapter. For example, if you are interested in South Africa, you look it up in Table 2.1 and you will find that it is a self-focused, high-power-differential country. If you look at this profile at the end of Chapter 4 on effective communication, you will find the typical type of communication used in South African companies.

We add a slight caution for the reader who is reading this type of book for the first time. As you read Chapters 2 and 3, you will come across a number of new terms that are that are critical to this book. When these ideas are first presented, they are explained fully using examples. In addition, we refer to these ideas often and provide reminders of what they mean as we use them later in the book. While the terms themselves might be unfamiliar, their meanings are not. As you come across these ideas in Chapters 2 and 3, give yourself a few extra moments to take note of them.

Finally, our purpose is not to present the information that you will need to become an "expert" on a given country. We will furnish the tools you need to operate in a variety of countries and cultures, but for country-specific information and details, you will need to turn to other sources. At the book's end, we have provided a number of general sources of country-specific information for topics ranging from politics to food to language.

Summary

The main objective of our book is to help you develop an innovative method of managing your employees. Integrating cultural diversity and values, this is a person-oriented approach to work. In addition, it is more than just a guide for the multinational manager since the foundation of our book, self-knowledge, can be used in any diverse work context. Therefore, a manager who works only within the United States can benefit as much from our recommendations as one working for a multinational corporation in Hong Kong, Australia, or Poland.

Quite simply put, we know of no other existing approach that enables a manager to understand his or her employees regardless of their cultural, racial, or ethnic backgrounds. In the following chapters, we will help you recognize the relationship between personal and cultural values, managerial practices, and work outcomes. Our approach explains why different managerial techniques are developed in different countries and the ways a manager might predict which will work best. As a result, a manager will understand not only the values that influence employees' actions but also the key values that shape *her or his own management style*. We now turn to the critical beginning for becoming a more effective global manager.

I

Understanding Yourself and Different Cultures

2

Understanding
Who You Are

One way to develop a new way of thinking about managing employees in a multicultural world is by questioning existing management approaches and seeing what has been useful and what has been left out. We have questioned existing approaches in an attempt to discover the beginning of the thread that would weave a new outlook on multicultural management in the global enterprise. In particular, we have made two assumptions: first, a person-oriented approach is fundamental to a comprehensive integration of cultural influences in the workplace; and, second, there exists a need to create a bridge between the general work environment and an individual employee's needs and values.

We begin our discussion by assuming that a person-oriented approach is a necessary, if not sufficient, way to talk about global management. An approach that takes into consideration a person's own values and needs is an essential starting point for understanding how abstract influences such as culture and society might influence an employee's actions. A person-oriented approach enables us to understand how people's experiences in their companies and social lives are processed and used as a basis for work activity. In this regard, an individual's culture is viewed as a shared way of acting that various members of the society use in day-to-day life. As such, culture serves as a way of judging the meaning of various managerial techniques and the value of their effects on workplace activity. For example, a British shop-floor worker may expect a degree of animosity between a manager and a worker, whereas a Saudi Arabian worker does not. Culture shapes the meaning of varied aspects of the workplace, including reward schemes, job environment, and promotion opportunities; it helps shape our choices by telling us what to value and what not to value.

Our second assumption is that it is difficult but absolutely necessary to connect the person-oriented approach to the general work environment. Without the integration of an employee's self-knowledge and revelations into a general work context, we have a tree but no forest. More than that, we don't even know what a tree really is and why we should care about it. People sort through their social and work worlds using their sense of self. If you are serious about learning the nature of managing in the global environment, you need to begin with understanding who you are and why you react as you do. For example, by knowing that employees from a group-focused country like Japan define their sense of self-worth through their work group's and company's accomplishments, you are able to make better judgments concerning the introduction of a company-based reward scheme such as employee stock ownership plans (ESOPs) in such a country. As such, a person's self-knowledge provides the link that can connect cultural values and management practices. This chapter describes in detail our cultural self-knowledge approach to management and provides a way to assess your self-motives and cultural values.

Figure 2.1 *A cultural self-knowledge approach to managing*

Key Pieces to Effective Global Management

We call our method of managing diversity the *cultural self-knowl-edge* approach, and it consists of four basic parts.[1] These are illustrated in Figure 2.1:

- Self-knowledge, or who we are as unique individuals
- Cultural values, or the shared way that certain groups have of seeing the world
- Managerial techniques, or the way that management practices contribute to a person's self-worth and well-being
- Work activity, or various ways of viewing outcomes such as productivity, organizational citizenship, absenteeism, and a positive attitude toward work leading to workplace commitment (buy-in) and job satisfaction

By *self-knowledge,* we mean that every single person has a unique set of motives that energize action. These motives make up each person's own psychological "fingerprint." In addition, there are cultural, or general, values that a person shares with others from his or her culture, social groups, organization, and the like; these values can be described by the consistent way these people view the world. Managerial techniques, of course, refer to the practices used by managers as they relate to personal and cultural factors. If these various elements are in harmony, then the work activity that results is positive and beneficial. Otherwise problems may arise, and the workplace becomes unproductive.

The potential usefulness of various managerial practices and motivational techniques depends on cultural values and norms. For example, managerial practices that reward personal competition may be highly valued in an individualistic culture such as Australia but not in a collectivistic one like Vietnam or Singapore. A supervisor who encourages open criticism will be appreciated by employees in a culture of low power differentials (in which employees feel free to exchange ideas with their bosses) such as Sweden, but she or he will raise the suspicion of employees in a culture of high power differentials like Mexico. Is it any wonder that the authoritarian style of the Japanese manager (high power differentials) is often met with resistance and resentment from U.S. (low power differentials) automobile workers in U.S.-Japan joint ventures?

Yet, understanding how cultural values relate to management practices is only part of the story. After all, employees interpret the meaning and value of various managerial techniques in relation to their personal needs as well. They approve of managerial practices that provide opportunities for accomplishing personal goals and for experiencing self-worth. We now turn to a discovery of a person's psychological fingerprint, or self-knowledge.

Self-Knowledge

Although people differ in many ways, there are a number of basic characteristics that they share regardless of their national, ethnic, religious, or racial backgrounds. Self-knowledge is a composite view that an individual forms through personal experiences and those values adopted from people who are important to that person. Self-knowledge is developed through our childhood and adulthood experiences and by examination of the world around us.

Each person's psychological fingerprint is the complex set of memories, thoughts, ways of thinking, and feelings about the world. A person's self-knowledge refers to a complex way that we define ourselves, and it consists of many roles that we may occupy (such as manager, parent, or golf partner) as well as the specific characteristics that mark our specific traits (such as a liking for spicy Chinese food or a quick wit). People differ in these character-istics and in their relative importance. In other words, if you think about the seasoning on food as a "dimension" of the self, you can see that everyone has a desire for some spices but that some peo-ple like lots of salt, some jalapeño peppers, and some sweet sauces.

The various pieces that make up our self-knowledge are orga-nized in a general hierarchy that helps us understand new experi-ences more efficiently. For example, a manager who places a strong emphasis on central control and authority may easily set aside a secondary characteristic of friendliness to subordinates if an employee has made a mistake or violated company policy. Con-trarily the manager who places friendliness above an autocratic style may avoid conflict and criticism of a poorly performing subor-dinate.

The amount of information included in our self-knowledge is enormous, including our past and present experiences and our anticipated future ones.[2] However, not all this information is rele-vant all of the time. The parts of our self-knowledge brought to our attention at any particular moment is determined by the particular work environment that we are experiencing. This part of our thoughts that is active at any moment is called the working self, or the self-knowledge of the moment. It is this working self that helps us directly confront the world. Compared to deeper levels of self-knowledge, our working self is more accessible, active, mal-leable, and tied to current events. The nature of our immediate work environment determines what characteristics of self-knowledge are in the working self. For instance, if we show up to work and everyone is in a festive mood because of an upcoming holiday, our thoughts may be drawn to our past holiday experiences and we will be festive as well.

There are three universal motives that guide our self-knowledge. By understanding these and the processes that guide their satisfaction, we can gain important insights into why our subordinates work and react the way that they do. Also we can determine the most effective way to manage employees who come from diverse backgrounds or cultures. The three motives are:

- *Self-enhancement,* or a desire to feel good about ourselves and keep a positive self-image
- *Self-growth,* or a desire to see ourselves as competent and capable of facing new challenges
- *Self-consistency,* or a desire to sense and experience coherence and continuity in our lives

The self-enhancement motive is quite simple—people always want to feel positive and good about themselves and will do things to enhance their self-image.[3] The experience of self-enhancement is affected by opportunities in the work environment (and elsewhere). What is important but less obvious is that the *source* of what makes people feel good differs according to their general values. What makes a Chinese worker feel a sense of achievement may be very different from an American. James Wall, Jr., comments about Chinese management practices, "Quite often, managers bring family members to the work site emphasizing that productivity depends heavily on their family member. Whenever there is a promotion, the family not only is brought in, but is praised for its member's (i.e., its own) success."[4] Further, criticism in a Chinese enterprise is often dealt with through someone in the family's pointing out the worker's poor performance to other family members who in turn sanction the person and encourage better work habits. In the United States, an employee would see such management actions as an invasion of privacy and home.

There are a number of ways that a motive for self-enhancement influences how people think about the world. For instance, people have a general tendency to use the information that they are given about themselves in the most positive way possible. We can all likely recall a long performance review with a subordinate that consisted of many negative comments and perhaps one or two supportive ones. What that employee likely remembers after this long discussion are the one or two positive things, and she or he often interprets the negative in terms of the supportive comments ("a selective perception"). This type of reality distortion is quite natural since it helps the employee keep a good self-image. Another way to maintain a good feeling about self is by blaming our failures on reasons beyond our control. For example, an employee who is confronted with a failure to meet a deadline may point out that other people have missed similar deadlines, the time frame was unrealistic, or critical resources were unavailable. All of these excuses move the blame away from the person and back to explanations that do not threaten a person's self-enhancement. In other words, these excuses help a person protect their own image, and self-enhancement is the motive that drives such actions.

Self-growth is our belief that we can successfully complete a job or task and our interest in challenging ourselves in the future. People make these judgments all of the time as they think about trying to reach the sixteenth green with a two-iron versus a five-wood, if they can get that new job that is opening up in the marketing division, or if they can finish cutting the lawn before it rains. This important concept was developed by psychologist Albert Bandura, who argues that though people tend to avoid tasks and situations that they believe exceed their capabilities, they also enjoy challenging themselves as a way of improving their skills. Self-growth guides a people's choice of situations and activities toward ones likely to be mastered, and it eliminates activities that seem unachievable. This last point is very important because what a person *thinks* can be accomplished is as important as what can actually be achieved. As we will see in Chapter 6, effective leaders and managers are often people who can help raise their employees' self-growth to high levels. In reaching for the stars, we may fall short, but we may still reach the moon.

An effective manager can help raise an employee's growth to help him or her achieve goals thought to be impossible. For example, Gregory Northcraft, Terri Griffith, and Christina Shalley talk about CEO Sam Eichenfeld's muscle-building program at Greyhound Financial Corporation. One of the major aspects to the program is job rotation in which key executives swap jobs even if they are not functionally trained in the other area. The purpose of this program is to create a deeper pool of executive talent and to help important personnel understand their full potential. The authors point out: Muscle building is not temporary reassignment; it is a form of career alteration. Implicit in the program is the lack of a "safety net"—for either the individual or the company. Once jobs are swapped, a muscle builder has no job to fall back on if the new job doesn't work out. The old job is filled, usually by another muscle builder. Nor is the time horizon sufficiently short that a muscle builder can just try to "get through it." Thus, there is a strong incentive for a muscle builder to excel and contribute in the new function and it is important for GFC to identify muscle builders who will adapt and succeed.[5]

People develop their sense of self-growth from four general sources, including

- *Prior successes,* based on authentic mastery experiences. Past successes raise a person's self-growth whereas repeated failures lower them.
- *Learning by watching others* is another factor that affects self-growth. Visualizing other people performing success fully positively affects a person's own self growth.
- *Verbal persuasion,* or telling people that they are capable, is the third factor that either enhances or inhibits self-growth.
- *Physical state,* or a person's general well-being, serves as a basis for evaluating one's capability.

One example of how people's work situations might influence their sense of growth is presented in work by Dov Eden, who has documented what he calls the Pygmalion Effect. This effect is illustrated in the popular play *My Fair Lady,* based on George Bernard Shaw's *Pygmalion* adapted from Greek mythology.[6] The theme is quite simple: a person's expectations of others will influence how she or he acts toward them, and this behavior in turn influences how they respond. For instance, if a manager is confident that an employee is capable and competent, the former will often give the later the benefit of the doubt, provide the employee with challenging opportunities, and make certain that he or she has adequate resources to get a job done. Naturally, if an employee is given all of these opportunities, that individual is likely to be successful, and this success then strengthens the manager's view that the employee is capable, and so on. However, if a manager doesn't think that an employee is not very competent, the employee will get fewer challenging assignments, and any problems that arise will strengthen the manager's view that "he wasn't up to the work anyway." Thus, if people place expectations on certain groups of employees, (e.g., women or underrepresented groups), the result may be a self-fulfilling prophecy, or getting back exactly what was expected.

The concept of self-growth has mainly focused on the single employee. However, a sense of *group growth* is crucial for what people choose to do together, how much effort they put into joint projects, and how persistent they are when facing failures. The strength of groups, organizations, and nations lies partly in people's sense of group growth. We don't know exactly how group growth is influenced by a person's culture, but some recent management research suggests some patterns. We believe that people's culture shapes their individual and group growth. In a group-focused culture such as Japan and Sweden, with their history of effective teamwork, group growth is higher than in a group-focused culture like Russia, which has a history of variable success. Also we often find that group growth is lower in a self-focused than in a group-focused culture. This difference arises because self-focused cultures have a more limited experience with teamwork, so they are less likely to have a history of group successes.

While we know a lot about the motives of self-enhancement and self-growth, the motive of *self-consistency* and its role in everyday life is more unclear.[7] A sense of continuity and consistency helps people to connect their current experiences to past ones and to maintain a coherent picture of themselves. Such a coherent view is necessary for operating effectively in the environment. In some sense, people's sojourns to "find themselves" or to "get in touch" with their feelings is a reflection of disrupted consistency. Self-consistency is what helps people understand what is happening to them in terms of what has happened in the past, and it guides their future actions. Imagine if a person's job was new every day, and that individual never had any of the same friends at work! How would the person know how to act and whom to trust? People feel most comfortable when they have at least some consistency in their work and friends.

The motive for self-consistency has a number of effects on how people act. First, it leads people to interpret new experiences in terms of past ones. This process occurs as people organize their memories (e.g., inconsistent experiences are often distorted or forgotten). An employee used to being told what to do by an autocratic boss may have a great deal of trouble adjusting to one who encourages participation. Likewise, work groups that have had flexible schedules may react poorly to rigid work shifts, even to the point of denying that such changes have occurred in their company. Second, self-consistency directs people to act according to the values that they have adopted and live by. It is no wonder that it is very difficult to retrain managers to empower their employees if they have traditionally used an autocratic management style. Not only does the company need to train its managers how to empower their subordinates but it also has to retrain their way of thinking.

In a very direct fashion, a person's motive for self-consistency will affect the perceived legitimacy of various managerial techniques. Techniques that are consistent with the traditions and norms and that are familiar to an employee are more likely to be accepted than others. This factor may add to our understanding of why certain techniques are more effective than others.

Where Does Self-Knowledge Come From?

Increasingly we have come to the realization that our self-knowledge must function within a particular environment and that there is no meaningful way to speak about people removed from where they work and live. In other words, people are incomplete and therefore unable to live fully unless they are in their own community. Our enduring commitments to various people and groups helps us to define our self-knowledge.

All three self-motives—enhancement, growth, and consistency—are part of a person's self-knowledge, and they are affected by our goals and personal evaluations. People use two sources of evaluation for determining whether or not their self-motives have been satisfied:[8]

- *Independent-self* as determined by personal standards
- *Interdependent-self* as determined by the impressions received from others who are important to that person

The most important point is that these sources of self-knowledge that we pay attention to are modified by our cultural values. The self is active and leads a person to use varying sources of information and thus to act differently. Put another way, people look to different sources of evaluation, and in different amounts, across cultures. Those who are from a self-focused country like England use the independent self as a source of assessing their self-motives. In such a country, people pay attention to their unique talents, and they look for opportunities to express their individuality. In a group-focused countries like Mexico or Brazil, people look to their groups for information to shape their self-knowledge. People in a group-focused country are more attentive to comparisons with fellow group members that can strengthen their identification with their group.

People from the Pacific Rim pay most of their attention to group evaluations as the source of their self-knowledge, and western Europeans and North Americans look to self-evaluations the most. What does this mean from a more practical perspective? Let's take as an example some research conducted by the first author of this book looking at job training in the United States and mainland China. In working with telecommunications service representatives, he found that job feedback about a work group's performance was more useful in building a Chinese employee's confidence (self-growth motive) than feedback about the employee's personal performance. However, the opposite was true for the U.S. employees. The Chinese were looking to their work group as a source of information concerning their job success, whereas the Americans evaluated themselves by comparing themselves to their own internal standards. Earlier we quoted from James Wall, Jr., who talked about Chinese managers who use a worker's family to motivate or punish an employee. His description is consistent with our discussion because the family is clearly an important reference group for a Chinese employee. Thus a person's self-motives are influenced by the dominant source of self-knowledge. What is the strongest factor influencing that source? Cultural values.

Countries and Cultural Values

When we visit another country, another city, or even another community in our own city, we often see that people seem to think about things differently, eat different food, and live in very different ways. Not only do they seem to view the world in another way, but their assumptions about what is right and wrong may vary dramatically from our own. For example, a friend once described an interview that her friend had with an Israeli immigration official. He asked the friend to state her religious affiliation, to which question she replied, "Atheist." The official paused for a moment, and then again asked her to state her religious affiliation. Again she replied simply, "Atheist." Finally the official, who had grown impatient snapped, "Okay, what type of atheist are you—a Jewish atheist, a Muslim atheist, or a Christian atheist?"

The sharing of many values and experiences gives rise to common viewpoints. John Steinbeck discusses this reality in his novel, *America and the Americans.*[9] Steinbeck says that there is something unique about Americans that leads to their immediate identification by people from other countries. An American can simply walk into a room of Europeans, for example, and can be identified before he or she says a single word. Why is this? What creates recognizable characteristics in such a diverse country as the United States?

Culture is the shared way a group of people view the world. North Americans value individual liberty, whereas the Swiss espouse conformity and conservatism. Germans keep casual acquaintances at arms length until they know them quite well, and Scandinavians do not show excessive emotion. Are these stereotypes? Do these characteristics constitute "culture?" When thinking about culture, we get ourselves into trouble if we assume that the shared characteristics of a group of people *dictate entirely* how they behave.

One of the first lessons that the global manager must learn is that a person's actions are *guided, but not dictated,* by cultural values. While many Japanese workers value group activities, others prefer to work alone. Likewise, some Nigerians prefer to work with family members, and others do not. If we think about the characteristics of a culture as being similar to aspects of personality, such as an outgoing nature, it becomes clear that just as not everyone is outgoing, not everyone is group-oriented in a group-oriented country. As we discuss how cultural values operate in a company, it is therefore important to realize that these may not be identical for all people in a single country. At the same time, we would expect that people coming from the same country will exhibit some of the same general tendencies and think about things in a similar way.

Culture exists at various levels, ranging from a group to an organizational, to a national level. This idea is captured by Edgar Schein, who describes culture as "what a group learns over a period of time as that group solves its problems of survival in an external environment and its problem of internal integration."[10] Following this definition, any stable group of people having shared experiences can have a unique "culture," so within one nation there can be many subcultures. For example, American Telephone and Telegraph is renown for its strong hierarchy and chain-of-command. In describing AT&T practices, Richard Pascale relates the story of the former chairman of AT&T who required all of his top executives to live close to the corporate headquarters in case "the troops" had to respond to a crisis.[11] The AT&T "troops" adhered to a strict dress code, and their behavior during nonwork hours was as carefully regulated as their actions during work. In sharp contrast, Bill Gates's Microsoft Corporation is known for its informal (albeit high-pressure) style with many key personnel coming to work in casual attire and keeping flexible work hours. Once a group holds common assumptions about how the world works, people in the group are more likely to respond similarly to new events.

For some groups, the values that people hold are relatively consistent, and they form what we call *tight* cultures. However, some groups vary a great deal in their views of the world and do not hold the same values. Consequently they form a *loose* culture.[12] The strength and consistency of values held by people in a given culture are a function of the variety within a group, the length of time the group has worked together, the intensity of the group's experiences, and the generalizability of the norms for behavior across situations. Loose cultures seem to be more tolerant of individual initiative, whereas people from tight cultures are more intolerant.

Some people talk about culture by breaking it into specific facets or dimensions. We now turn to a discussion of two very important aspects of culture—namely, the way that people relate to themselves and groups, and the amount of power it is acceptable for people to have over others. We refer to the first dimension as a self versus a group focus; the second dimension refers to the power differentials found in a country.

How Do People Relate to One Another?

One of the most important ways to think about culture is whether or not an employee is *self-focused* or *group-focused*. People who are self-focused look to themselves to judge their actions, are introspective, and think about their personal goals and actions. People who are group-focused look to others as a way of judging their actions, and they think about how their activities relate to the consequences for their work group. The connection between who we are, and the people around us, is based on a number of consistent rules and principles that serve to guide a person's focus on goals and outcomes. As Amitai Etzioni points out, "Man is not unless he is social; what he is depends on his social being, and what he makes of his social being is irrevocably bound to what he makes of himself. He has the ability to master his internal being, *and the main way to self-mastery leads to his joining with others like himself in social acts.*"[13]

A self-versus a group focus refers to the connections that people have to their various social memberships, work groups, or clans. In self-focused cultures like the United States, people live in limited family relationships consisting of an "immediate family" such as husband, wife, and children. Grandparents will often live independently until some point that they can no longer care for themselves, after which they may move into a retirement community. Even the traditional nuclear family is evolving in the United

States, with increasing use by parents of day care for their children and more single-parent families. In group focused cultures like South Korea, Taiwan, Vietnam and Malaysia, the "immediate family" includes grandparents, uncles, aunts, cousins, or even close friends. These relationships can be determined by bloodlines or ties to distant relatives.

Of course, the United States and Vietnam are two ends of a continuum, and a number of countries such as France, Germany, and Spain, fall in between these two extremes. These countries reflect both characteristics of the group and self-focus. For instance, German management practices reflect an emphasis on collective action at a national level (through the labor-management system called codetermination) while maintaining an emphasis on individual reward systems and incentives. As we discuss various cultural examples, we will emphasize the extremes to clarify our points, however, we want to emphasize that more moderate cultures will share characteristics of both a self- and a group-focused culture.

In the workplace, a self- versus a group-focus can be used to talk about how employees relate to one another. Employees who are group- rather than self-focused, think about themselves as part of the team or group, put their team's goals ahead of their own goals, are concerned about the integrity of their team, and have an intense emotional attachment to their team or group. For example, Japanese workers do not fear how a poor performance makes them look personally; rather, they are concerned with how their own performance reflects on their work group. In contrast, employees in a self-focused country define themselves by personal actions, emphasize personal goals, and are willing to let go of work group attachments and commitments if they become personally troublesome.

It is important to remember that though one focus may dominate, the other exists to some degree as well. Some people living in a self-focused country may be very loyal and attached to their work groups and some from a group-focused country may pay most of their attention to their own work goals. Anthropologist Margaret Mead said that all societies are both competitive and cooperative, but what distinguishes among them is the relative balance of these two influences.[14] Likewise, all societies are both self-and group-focused; what distinguishes them is the balance between these two orientations. Of course, this is why we find that the Japanese team orientation for manufacturing can be useful at times in the United States since the self-focused Americans are quite able to work in teams so long as they do not threaten the personal goals of each team member. In such a case, the team member may seek out a new work group that can satisfy this or her personal needs.

How Acceptable Is It to Have Power and Status?

Another important aspect of culture that has important implications for the work place is what Geert Hofstede calls power distance,[15] or what we will refer to as *power differentials*. People from a low-power-differential culture do not believe that it is acceptable for one person to order another about, and they expect to have input concerning company policies that are important to them. A worker from Singapore (a very high-power-differential country) will not question an order from a superior even if the order is unexpected and places a heavy burden on the employee. This is not true for an employee from a low-power-differential country like Norway.

We can think about the power differences between people in various countries as related to their self- or group focus, but these are not the same thing. For instance, Japan is a country in which there is both a strong group focus as well as a high power differential; Sweden also has a strong group focus, but it has a very low power differential. Therefore a certain focus does not imply a particular power differential. Taken together, however, these two parts of culture help us understand the worldwide variation in people's values.

Mapping Out Cultural Values and the World

As an organizing tool, we summarize a number of examples of countries that range from low to high individual focus as well as low to high power differentials in Table 2.1. While this table does not include every country, it shows nations from every major region of the world. If a particular country that you are interested in is not listed, just choose another that is geographically close, and your country will likely be fairly similar. Throughout the book, if we refer to a low- or high-power-differential culture, you can refer to this table to see examples of such countries.

These important cultural values have direct implications for a person's self-knowledge. People from a self- or group-focused country think about and react to different information in their world. Japanese employees from Sony Corporation not only get rewarded through company-level incentives but also prefer them. People from a high-power-differential culture do not expect to participate in decision making or have a great deal of discretion in their work,

Table 2.1

*Examples of Countries and Culture Profiles with
Example Management Practice*

		Example Countries	Example Management Technique: Motivation Practices
Self-focus	Low power differential	Australia Canada Britain Finland Iceland Ireland New Zealand United States	Job design based on individual initiave and responsibility
	High power differential	Austria Belgium France Germany Italy Luxemborg Netherlands South Africa Spain Thailand	Work focusing on individual placed within a well-defined authority structure (bureaucratic)
Group-focus	Low power differential	Costa Rica Czech Republic Israel Jamaica Norway People's Republic of China Poland Russia Sweden Switzerland Taiwan	Team-based work with equality among group members
	High power differential	Brazil Egypt Greece India Indonesia Japan Malaysia Mexico Pakistan Peru Portugal Saudi Arabia Singapore South Korea Vietnam Venezuela	Team-based work with strong overview by superiors

whereas people from a low-power-differential culture expect and demand such opportunities. In other words, culture shapes us by reflecting what the world gives us as well as what we expect from it.

Assessing Self-Motives and Cultural Values

Taken together, these three motives and two cultural values provide us with an important understanding of what directs our actions and how we interpret the world. These views shape how we choose to work with our subordinates, peers, and superiors; and they are essential for us truly to appreciate how culture influences a person's actions in the workplace. We have developed a tool allowing a manager to assess self-motives and general cultural values. The cultural values include a self-versus a group focus as well as power differential; these are important for understanding where an individual will seek out information about self-knowledge.

This tool, listed in the Appendix can be used by you and your employees. The essential point to keep in mind is that this tool helps you know which of these motives are active for you and your subordinates as well as the relative level of each motive. The tool is also effective in determining *where and how* a person gets information concerning the self-motives. As we explained earlier, the source of these motives is a very important link for learning how cultural diversity influences people's actions.

To use the assessment tool, simply turn to the Appendix and complete the questionnaires following the instructions provided. The first questionnaire, "Assessing Your Cultural Values," is used to determine a manager's likely knowledge sources, and it consists of two parts. This tool helps a manager understand if she or he has a stronger self- or group-focus in general beliefs and values. After a total score for each of the cultural value scales is computed, turn to the "sample cultures" sheet (Table 2.1) to see where these scores fall in relation to people from other countries. Remember, the scores of people from the same country will vary because everyone's beliefs are unique and individual. In general, people who are high on the self- versus group-focus scale are more group-oriented, and they will seek information about their actions based on the reactions of groups important to them. The second scale measures the acceptability of power and status differences. People who are high on the power scale are very compliant to their superiors and do not question authority. They accept hierarchy as an important and inevitable part of work. For instance, Malaysian, Singaporean, and Thai workers are generally high on this scale, and their actions are likely to be consistent with their managers' orders and expectations. Therefore, if these managers want to shape the actions of their employees, they need to work through the existing chain-of-command rather than simply relying on informal, casual discussions with an employee. In addition, Japanese workers also are likely to be high on the power scale, a result suggesting that the supervisor's feedback is very important to the worker. Taken together with the Japanese group-focus value, this information implies that Japanese managers can effectively guide the work actions of their employees through feedback given to the work group.

The second part of the questionnaire consists of three parts corresponding to the three self-motives (enhancement, growth, and consistency). After filling out and scoring these subscales, you can determine which of the motives are most important. Again, you may find that more than one motive is very important and that these scores may actually change across time and situations. For instance, you may have a strong motive for consistency as well as a strong one for enhancement, an outcome suggesting that you will tend to seek out stable work situations in which recognition for personal actions can be gained. Other people may be low on enhancement but high on consistency. These persons may want a stable, low-profile job in which they do not get looked at "from above" very much. Other people have a low-consistency and high-growth motive, and they are likely to seek out a lot of work variety and often tackle difficult or even impossible challenges.

Summary

We have focused on the general characteristics of countries and cultures. Two key aspects of culture—self- versus group-focus and power differentials—were described as a way of understanding various countries. Our approach uses these general values and matches them to a person's unique self-knowledge.

At this point, you have now grasped the pieces of our self-knowledge approach to managing in a range of countries and cultures. However, a clear knowledge of your personal self-motives and cultural values is only a beginning. In the next chapter, we will show how you can take this understanding and determine the self-knowledge and cultural values of your subordinates in order to manage them more effectively.

3

Putting the Pieces Together

Armed with your new understanding of self-knowledge and cultural values, you are ready to investigate and determine the best way for you to manage others. Without question, the next step is to examine how self-knowledge and cultural values fit together and to determine the profiles of your subordinates so that a match (or mismatch) can be identified. In addition, these profiles will help you understand whether or not a particular management technique (e.g., management by objectives, job redesign) will be consistent with the orientation of employees. If it is not, you must take steps to change the profile of the subordinates (perhaps through special job training) or choose a different management style.

In this chapter, we describe a multistep plan for using our approach in your current work situation. We will help you choose the right management style for you. We draw on the topic of employee motivation as a way of illustrating our points.

Bringing the Key Ideas Together

The two sources of a person's self-knowledge—independent self (looking within yourself) and interdependent self (looking to others around you)—and the three self-motives—enhancement, growth, and consistency—were described as two separate systems in Chapter 2. The connection between these suggestions is the way national culture influences each employee's work habits. Where a person seeks self-knowledge dictates, in part the actions and situations that individual pays attention to in determining who he or she is, and these sources are influenced by cultural values. We show how these three facets fit together in Figure 3.1.

Let us take as an example situations and managerial practices that provide opportunities for individual success such as MBO or bonus schemes. In a self-focused country like Australia or Britain, these practices are evaluated in a positive fashion by the independent self. In other words, Australian workers who have a strong enhancement motive respond well to individual bonus schemes because they can get personal recognition for their accomplishments. However, enhancement in a group-focused country operates differently. There as we have seen, employees look to their work groups in order to evaluate themselves. In the same way, motives for self-growth and consistency are tied to important sources within a person's culture.

Putting the two parts of the assessment tool together, we can see how a person's specific motive profile, combined with his or her cultural background, predicts what aspects of the workplace are important for employees. Self-focused employees who are from a country low in power differentials (like Sweden) seek out self-evaluations and standards as a way of judging things and reject a superior who tries to give too many orders. For such employees,

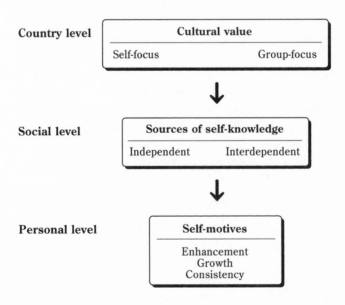

Figure 3.1 *The interplay of self-knowledge source and motives of the self*

Table 3.1

Culture Profiles of Employees

	High power differential	Low power differential
Self-focus	Entrepreneur	Oldest child
	Answers to self and likes to break rules to get things done	Answers to self but responds to authority and has strong sense of duty
Group-focus	Collective rebel	Model citizen
	Endorses what the group thinks is important and sacrifices for the group but rejects rules and strong leader figures	Supports the group fully and accepts the hierarchy and leadership that exists in and outside the group

neither participation nor direct control is useful since the employees respond to internal standards and question authority. Thus we have the following culture profiles illustrated in Table 3.1:

- Self-focus, low power differential. This person is the *entrepreneur* since she or he answers to personal standards and questions existing authority.
- Self-focus, high power differential. This person is the *oldest child* since she or he answers to personal standards but follows a sense of duty.
- Group-focus, lower power differential. This person is the *collective rebel* since she or he thinks about the group but rejects authority.
- Group-focus, high power differential. This person is the *model citizen* since she or he thinks about the group and follows a strong sense of duty.

Finally, if we combine these profiles with the various self-motives, we see that there are a variety of ways to implement various management techniques, but that they need to be congruent with employees' values. In Figure 3.2, we provide an example of employee profiles combining the self-motives and self- versus group-focused culture. What are these various employees like? At the top of the figure, the employees are from a self-focused country and in the bottom from a group-focused country. In each case, we give an example of people who are high or low on each of the self-motives. For instance, take the following three examples:

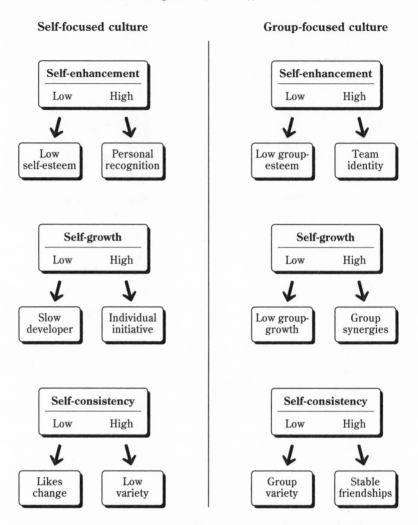

Figure 3.2 *Employee profiles combining self-motives and self- versus group-focused culture*

- A British (self-focused country) worker, Alfred, who has a high enhancement motive, high growth motive, and low consistency motive
- An British worker, Nigel, who has high enhancement, low growth, and high consistency motives
- A Mexican (group-focused country) worker, Benito, who has high enhancement, high growth, and low consistency motives

Alfred wants personal recognition, opportunities to take individual initiative, and a lot of change in his work. Nigel will also respond well to personal recognition, but he wants a relatively stable work environment that does not have too many new challenges. Benito pays attention to and seeks out group recognition, but he doesn't like individual recognition. He wants new work challenges and variety in his work group. What this figure illustrates is that knowing an employee's cultural background gives us only part of the story. In our example, Alfred and Nigel should not be treated the same way just because they are British. Nevertheless, for both of them, their motives are satisfied through individually focused management techniques. Likewise, knowing a person's self-motives is only part of the picture; Benito's motives are the same as Alfred's, but the two respond very differently to individual versus group-based rewards and recognition because of their different cultures. Implementing a new management technique therefore requires that the approach be tailored to employees' motives and cultural background.

Applying Self-Knowledge to Your Work Situation

An important point of Table 3.1 and Figures 3.1 and 3.2 is for you to understand how your personal and cultural profiles, as well as the profiles for your subordinates, match up with your managerial style. What does this match mean for managing more effectively? We have developed a five-step plan for a manager in determining what management techniques to use at work:

1. Determine the relative strength of the manager's self-motives and the motives of subordinates.
2. Determine the manager's type of culture the and that (or those) of subordinates.
3. Examine the type of managerial technique that the manager is considering to see how it matches (or fails to match) the motives and culture of the manager and subordinates.
4. If there is a match between a management technique and the subordinate's culture and motives, then apply it; otherwise, seek out a new technique.
5. Work on diversifying the manager's own motives and sources of self-knowledge so that the manager is better able to adapt to a diverse work force.

These steps are a beginning to effective management.

An example might help clarify these relationships. Take a U.S. manager with strong individual growth and enhancement motives who has recently been put in charge of a Brazilian subsidiary of her company. Coming from the United States, she has a strong tendency to use an independent self-knowledge source (she uses her own internal standards for judging her successes and failures). Her workers, however, are from a group-focused country in which interdependent self-knowledge sources are important. This situation alone would suggest that the U.S. manager must be careful to provide group-level feedback and to give work goals and job assignments consistent with a team orientation (being careful to make certain that the teams are naturally existing ones composed of people who are loyal to one another).

Yet, this is only part of the picture. The manager still needs to understand which self-motives seem to be most important to her subordinates. Let's say she finds out that the consistency motive is most important. What effect does this finding have? Well, if she comes in and immediately changes around work routines, job assignments, and so forth, she will be met with unusually high resistance. But why is it also important for her to know her *own* self-motives? She needs to understand what her own natural tendencies will be in selecting and implementing work practices for others. As we mentioned earlier, people often use the techniques with which they feel most comfortable, as guided by their own self-motives. Maybe our U.S. expatriate manager feels free to "shake things up a bit" by changing around the work setting and chain-of-command because she has a very low self-consistency motive (so change does not bother her at all). This might explain her initial actions in the Brazilian setting. A fundamental understanding of self-knowledge helps any manager realize why he or she prefers some techniques over others and why these may or may not be suitable in other countries.

Choosing the Right Management Style

Now that you know your (and your employees') self-motives and cultural values, let's determine some effective management techniques for you. We will discuss these techniques in much more detail at the end of each applications chapter, so the following is just a brief taste of what is to come.

As we have pointed out, managerial practices are evaluated according to their contribution to employee self-motives and well-being. Cultural values serve as criteria for assessing the potential contribution of management practices to employee self-knowledge. A positive evaluation results in a good effect on work outcomes. Thus self-knowledge helps us understand the *relationship* between managerial practices and important work outcomes.

One way to interpret the relative effectiveness of various managerial and motivational techniques is to place them into two basic categories: those consistent with a self-focused culture that provides people with opportunities for satisfying self-motives using the independent source; and those consistent with a group-focused culture that offer possibilities for the development of the self-motives using the interdependent source. Such a classification helps us align a number of managerial techniques with cultural characteristics.

Table 3.2 summarizes the classification of various managerial techniques into the two categories. Managerial techniques congruent with self-focused values—such as individual job enrichment, individual goal setting, and individual incentives—have been found to work best in self-focused countries such as Australia, Canada, Britain, and the United States.

In contrast, managerial techniques that correspond to group-focused values—such as quality circles, autonomous work groups, team goals, and participation in goal setting and decision making—have been found to work best in group-focused cultures such as Brazil, Italy, Japan, mainland China, and Vietnam.

Based on common sense, we can see that managerial techniques that relate to the cultural values of people are more likely to be accepted than others, and that motivational factors that are highly valued in certain cultures are more likely to contribute to self-knowledge than others. It is therefore reasonable to argue that more attention should be given to cultural values because they guide a person's evaluation of the self.

How well will the self-knowledge model work for you? An example from the field of leadership illustrates the value of our approach. Robert House and others have looked at the nature of

Table 3.2

Group versus Self-Focused Managerial Techniques

Technique	Self-focused	Group-focused
Goal-setting	Individual goals	Team goals
Incentives	Individual	Group
Performance appraisal	Individual	Group or company-based
Job design	Job enrichment	Autonomous work groups and quality circles
Communication	Low interpersonal	High interpersonal
Problem solving	Individually based	Group-based
Decision-making	Majority vote	Group consensus

charismatic leadership and its effects on the self-concept of followers.[1] They have found that charismatic leaders have the ability to empower their followers by identifying the factors that increase their sense of self-enhancement and self-growth. The effective leader increases the motivation of followers by emphasizing the importance of their effort in attaining the leader's goals.

The relationship between culture and the efficacy of different managerial techniques has been scrutinized in a number of scientific investigations. For example, John French found that in Norway it was legitimate to have union representatives participate in decision making but not the employees themselves. Since direct participation did not conform to established work norms, it was not effective. Similarly the first author of this book found that in the Dunlop Tire Corporation, British shop stewards were more highly trusted than supervisors by shop-floor workers. As a result, their decisions were more accepted by British than by U.S. workers.[2]

The effectiveness of participation on employees' commitment and performance is influenced by values in their culture. Group participation depends on group-focused values and on a low power difference between a supervisor and a subordinate. Indeed, we have compared the effectiveness of participation in Israel, a group-focused culture, with that in the United States, a self-focused culture. We found that the Israelis reacted adversely to being assigned a performance goal as opposed to one determined using participation. Israelis who were assigned goals were less committed to them and performed less well, than Israelis who participated in goal setting. Such differences, however, were not observed for the Americans.

Another example can be raised in relation to team goals and performance. Tamao Matsui of Surugadin University and his colleagues in Japan have found that team goals are successful for Japanese people.[3] Yet, in self-focused cultures like Australia or the United States, team goals very often result in slacking off and free riding because members do not share responsibility to the same extent as those in group-focused cultures. As a result, team performance can be a problem in a self-focused country like the United States unless people are held personally accountable for their actions.

Differences in self- versus group-focused values may explain why different models of job enrichment have been developed in the United States as compared with Norway, Sweden, or Japan. In the United States Richard Hackman of Harvard University and Greg Oldham of the University of Illinois have developed a widely implemented model of job enrichment that focuses on the redesign of jobs for the individual employee.[4] Although their approach encompasses many critical aspects of a person's job, the model does not include self-knowledge dimensions that relate to a group evaluation source of information such as the formation of social relationships and support. In contrast, North European countries like Sweden and Norway have adopted models of autonomous work groups; North European countries are known to have more group-focused values than the United States. In Japan, job redesign has taken the form of quality control circles that coincide with the group-focused culture. In fact, the whole system of interpersonal communication and decision making in Japan is designed to correspond to group-focused values, including small-group activities at all organizational levels.

It is clear that the differences in effectiveness of managerial techniques across countries is not a coincidence. Rather, these reflect the patterns of personal and cultural values that we have identified in our model of self-knowledge.

Summary

Our model of cultural self-knowledge proposes that the potential effectiveness of various managerial techniques is based on the self-motives of individuals and where they seek information about their self-motives. The source of our self-motives lies in our cultural backgrounds; people from a group-focused culture will look to their work groups and families as a way of assessing their successes and failures, whereas people from a self-focused culture will look to their own internal standards. In addition, managerial techniques that reward people's contributions to their group work best in group-focused countries, whereas techniques that emphasize the individual (e.g., reward systems for individual performance) are more useful in self-focused countries. Therefore we can use our model to determine why various managerial techniques are not consistently effective in all cultures.

What should be stressed as well is that we are talking about *cultural* not just *national* diversity. A manager wanting to motivate people in a United States plant with a strictly American work force can use these principles of self-knowledge just as well as the expatriate traveling to Mexico City or Taipei or Nice to start up a new joint venture. Cultural diversity means that employees don't share the same cultural values and beliefs. What our model provides is a blueprint for understanding how people differ and why they may react as they do to various aspects of their workplace. The exposure to various cultures and subcultures also sharpens managers' awareness to their own self-knowledge as part of the comparisons they make. The next step is to take these fundamental principles and apply them to real management problems. In the next four chapters, we turn to the challenge of applying cultural self-knowledge to the specific management topics of communication, teamwork, leadership, and quality production management. In each of these chapters, we offer a specific approach using our cultural self-knowledge model.

II

Applying
Self-Knowledge to
Management

4

Did You Understand
What I Said?

The last two decades witnessed for a telecommunication systems revolution. An increasing number of people rely on electronic mail, fax, cellular phones, and teleconference equipment to communicate inside and across corporate and national borders. Some of the most recent technological developments are the information superhighway, wireless communication (including cellular phones), and digital cellular and personal communication networks (PCNs).[1] This new technology is building "anytime, anywhere" communication, creating the *wireless world,* as illustrated in Figure 4.1.

Does this revolution reflect personal communication, mutual understanding, and harmony, or is it only an illusion of stronger person-to-person connections? Does it strengthen the feeling of togetherness, or is it mainly a network of intelligent machines, computers, technically interconnected by electric pulses? It seems that the answers to these questions depend to a large extent on culture. The smooth flow of communication relies not only on the availability of communication channels but also on the ability to interpret correctly the content of information.

In this chapter, we will discuss the basics of how people communicate in a variety of cultures and nations. We begin by describing the *communication process* as a sharing of information and ideas among two or more people. Next we discuss the amount of communication found throughout a number of countries and then we review styles of communication there. Finally, we contrast several countries' styles of communication in modern organizations,

Building Blocks for the Wireless World

*Some of the technologies being
developed for a new era of communications*

Digital Cellular

By moving from today's analog system to new digital technology, cellular phone-system capacity will expand dramatically,
and data communications via cellular will become easier

Personal Communications Networks, or PCNs

A system of cheap pocket phones using "microcell"
radio transmissions that eventually could replace wired
phones, even in the home

Satellite Phones

These systems, such as Motorola's proposed Iridium
service, would ring the earth with low-orbit satellites to
connect calls to any point on the globe

Cellular Digital Packet Data

An enhancement planned for today's analog cellular phone
systems to allow "packets" of data—electronic mail, for
example—to "hop" between temporarily free voice channels

Packet Radio

These sustems, such as Ardis from IBM and Motorola and
Ram Mobile Data from BellSouth and Ram Broadcasting,
allow two-way, data-only communications to handheld devices

Personal Communicators

The first models, such as those from AT&T/EO and Apple
Computer, appear this year. Think of them as mobile PCs
of the wireless age

Wireless Computer Networks

Linking PCs and other computers by radio wave eliminates
miles of costly, confusing cables and makes it much easier
to reconfigure systems

Figure 4.1 *Revolutionary telecommunication systems*

including the United States (self-focus, low power differential),
Japan (group focus, high power differential), France (self-focus,
high power differential), and the Czech Republic (group focus, low
power differential). We have chosen these countries because they
represent each of the four combinations of group versus self-focus
and low versus high power differentials (see Table 8.2 for a summary). While these countries each have unique characteristics,
they do represent cultural groupings, so the lessons learned from
one country will help out in others.

Effective Communication

Communication is a process of information exchange that begins with a source of information, a person who decides which message to send and what signals and symbols to use. The message is then transmitted through certain channels (such as a memo or E-mail) to a receiver, who decodes the information, interprets it, and acts accordingly. The information that comes to (the receiver) is processed according to a coding system shaped by that individual's knowledge, values, expectations, and motives. How well a message is understood depends on the extent to which the coding system is shared by both the sender and the receiver. This sense of sharing is anchored in culture. In other words, people from the same culture are more likely to use the same way of interpreting messages than people from different cultures. Common meaning enables people to comprehend each other's intentions and actions and to respond appropriately.

A key factor is understanding communication difficulties lies in identifying the rules that people use for interpreting situations and messages. Maryan Schall has studied the communication problems between two divisions of the same company—the information system department and the investment department.[3] Her analysis of the communication rules used in the company showed that both departments had a strong task focus and a sense of urgency. Both valued technical competence and performance achievements, and managers from both departments wanted to control key resources. However, there were significant differences in the meaning of urgency. Urgency in the information system department was associated with achieving long-term projects like networking the entire organization, whereas in the investment department it implied short-term, daily deadlines like producing income reports. To increase resource control, managers in the information system department built alliances within that department and with others; by contrast managers of the investment department increased resource control by personal involvement in day-to-day operations. Members of information systems valued the seeking and sharing of information. In the other department information flow was restricted to certain subgroups. When the two departments interacted, they thus faced problems of coordination and insufficient communication.

In addition to these differences, there were also issues involving communication between the managers and employees in both departments. Managers in the information system department gave first priority to meeting deadlines, whereas employees' first priority was to produce the highest quality possible. In the investment department, managers' first priority centered on coordinating efforts toward accomplishing group wide results; employees' priorities were focused on independent attempts to accomplish particular tasks and assignments. The respect of managers and employees toward one anothers' priorities was higher in the information system department than in the investment department. As a result, members of the investment department experienced frustration, tension, and a sense of alienation.

The case of these two departments suggests that there are two aspects of communication: it can be a process as well as a message. People who agree to communicate may sometimes disagree on the meaning of the information. Nevertheless, they continue to communicate. In case of disagreement they are willing to make a statement that they "agree to disagree", but nevertheless they continue to communicate and negotiate.

The need to bridge cultural differences in communication has been recognized by Intel, the multinational chip-manufacturing empire based in California. In Israel, Intel has three plants with over a thousand employees in chip design, manufacturing, and sales. There is a continuous flow of communication between the United States and Israel via E-mail, teleconferences, and faxes. In addition, there are frequent visits of Israelis to Intel United States and vice versa. In order to assure a smooth flow of communication across cultural borders the training department of Intel has developed a workshop that trains employees for the United States-Israel interface. The workshop consists of an examination of "Intel culture," a common denominator for all Intel employees. The company values emphasize results orientation, customer orientation, risk taking, quality, discipline, and quality of working life. The workshop identifies the cultural differences between the American and the Israeli cultures: Americans respect privacy, and Israelis highly value group membership. Americans emphasize personal achievement and responsibility; Israelis stress both personal and team achievement and responsibility. Americans like competition, and Israelis value status equality. The interpersonal style of the Israeli expresses sincerity, openness, directness, and informality, whereas the Americans show politeness, formality, and sensitivity to criticism. The workshop relates actual events of miscommunication that have happened in the company and allows the participants to discuss the reasons for misunderstanding. In addition, participants get a glossary of company terms to familiarize them with common on-site language. This workshop provides Intel employees with the basic knowledge and understanding that allow them to communicate across cultures and within the company.

This example, like the one of CTX in Chapter 2, clearly illustrates the importance of smooth communication to the successful working of a company. Cultural differences in communication exhibit themselves in level of intensity of communication, in style, in patterns of decision making, and in conflict resolution. Therefore familiarity with the cultural values helps avoid misunderstanding and improves communication. The following section examines how cultural values shape the different patterns of communication.

Amount and Type of Communication

Group-focused countries have tight social networks. In these cultures, to be a person means to be related to other people. In the Chinese language, the concept of being human is *"ren*; it is *jin"* in Japanese. These ideas reflect a person's way of relating to other people. In contrast, self-focused countries have loose social networks that do not require strong connections among people. In the West, being human means having the qualities of man, as distinct from animals, without direct reference to others.

The low level of communication in the United States has been identified as one of the key managerial problems facing companies, according to a survey of 750,000 middle managers conducted by the Hay Group, a Philadelphia consulting firm. (Its clients have included American Airlines, Disney, General Electric, Chase Manhattan, and Maytag). In 1985, the Hay Group found that 85 percent of middle managers felt that information given to employees was satisfactory, by 1990, that figure had dropped to 69 percent.

Some successful American corporations have recognized the importance of communication. The late CEO Sam Walton of Wal-Mart used to say, "Communicate, communicate, communicate: If you have to boil down the Wal-mart system to one single idea, it would probably be communication because it is one of the real keys to our success."[3] Unlike the West, Japan and other group-focused cultures often put a strong emphasis on communication. Successful communication is necessary for maintaining their social networks. In group-focused countries, communication facilitates the sharing of cultural values and enhances the formation of tight cultures where everybody uses the same communication rules and correctly encodes and decodes information signals. Communication in Japan is valuable not only for the sharing of existing information but also for the creation of new information necessary for the continuous renewal process of organizations. As Ikujiro Nonaka of Hitotsubashi University puts it, modern organizations emphasize the role of information in creating knowledge.

Japanese corporations stress the importance creative ideas. To this end corporations like Shiseidu (Japan's largest cosmetic maker), Omron Corporation (a maker of electronic controls), and Simuzu Corporation (Japan's largest construction company), sponsor *soul-searching* programs. These consist of spending several days of company time each year at resort hotels to use philosophical introspection to make over a corporate culture. During the seminars, teams of employees and managers simulate situations where they tackle taxing problems, such as getting back from the moon on a damaged spacecraft. By taking this approach, Japanese companies hope both to improve existing products and methods, and also to come up with new technology and product developments.

Communication not only within, but also between, companies is becoming crucial in the competitive global market. If you run a big company, you face the challenge of getting things done faster. If you run a small one, you often struggle to find resources and do not have the in-house expertise to implement changes quickly and launch new products that satisfy the changing needs of the customers. The company of the future that will be able to adjust rapidly to changes in the markets is the *virtual corporation*. The virtual corporation is a temporary network of independent companies—suppliers, manufacturers, and distributors—linked by information technology to share skills, costs, and access to one another's markets. The virtual organization will have neither a central office nor an organizational chart. It will have horizontal integration rather than hierarchy. Each company that is linked to others will contribute only what it regards as its core competencies. The virtual organization will mix and match what each company does best. Partnerships and alliances are gaining greater importance for organizational competitiveness.

The case of TelePad demonstrates how the virtual organization operates. Ron Oklewicz, a veteran of Xerox and Apple Computer, founded TelePad two years ago to realize an idea he had for manufacturing pen-based computers. The computer was designed and codeveloped with GVO an industrial design company in Palo Alto, California. A team of experts from Intel was brought in to do the engineering work, and a battery maker collaborated to develop portable power supply. To manufacture the computer, the company is using spare capacity at an IBM plant in Charlotte, North Carolina. The pay checks for its fourteen employees are issued by an outside firm. Oklewicz himself brings in his experience in selling computers to the government.

The communication networks essential to virtual corporations are highly developed in Japan and in other cultures of the Pacific Rim, where they are fostered by the cultural characteristics of collective values and group orientation. Western organizations, which are anchored in self-focused cultures, should exert utmost effort to open up these strong communication networks inside and outside their corporations. While some large U.S. companies such as Exxon or Standard or USX may need to continue their horizontal and vertical existence, even these giants will benefit from increased communication flows and alliances in foreign markets—for example Exxon's work in tapping at the oil reserves in Siberia and elsewhere in Russia.

Styles of International Communication

We have observed that differences in cultural values lead to different communication styles. Vietnam, Brazil, Singapore, Japan, Korea, and China are known for their strong group orientation. In these cultures, the need to preserve group harmony can be seen in the communication style. Corporate communication in Japan is based on *personal, oral* communication, whereas in the West it often takes the form of written documents and electronic mail. Kosuke Kiyosy, general manager of International Operations of Tokyo Shobaru Electric, describes the differences in communication styles between Japanese and Americans: "In Japan, business is conducted in face-to-face discussions, not in letters. American businesses start out with sending letters, but to Japanese a letter is sort of record or conclusion. If you are dealing with a company in Japan and start by sending a letter, you will not get an answer.... When we have talked many times, then we will write letters as a record, as a confirmation. That is an entirely different way of doing business."[4]

Group-focused countries put more pressure on people to conform to the group; individuals cannot freely express their private selves. In Japan, there are two different facets of the self: *tatemae* which corresponds to the public self and entails behavior observable by anyone, and *honne* which corresponds to the private self and relates to private thoughts. Decisions in group-focused cultures are made by the group, not by a single decision maker. Individual

American managers who visit Japan for business purposes become frustrated when they encounter a group of Japanese who come to the meeting to negotiate business matters, as illustrated in Figure 4.2.

Japanese managers believe that harmony, or *wa,* leads to strength. Japanese managers who operate in the United States express their difficulties in explaining to Americans the importance of harmony. The latter are guided by self-focused values, rather than concern for group harmony. They are more likely to use explicit language for interpersonal communication ("absolutely," "certainly" and "positively"), regardless of whether the issue under discussion is acceptable to their counterparts or not.

The style of conducting meetings also differs between Japanese and Americans. Americans invite open and honest confrontation. The Japanese avoid such confrontation and tend to discuss disagreements prior to the formal meeting. In fact, the meeting provides a formal approval of a decision reached during informal consultations. Decisions in Japan are more often reached by consensus, whereas in the United States decisions are more often reached through the majority rule.

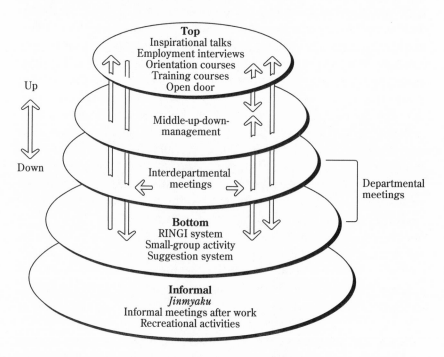

Figure 4.2 *Model of Japanese corporate communications system* (Erez 1992)

An emphasis on equality is another cultural characteristic that shapes our communication. In Singapore, a low level of equality is reflected in the hierarchical structure of companies. Communication is affected by status, age, and gender. Young people pay respect to old people, juniors to seniors, and low-level employees to higher managers. Age, seniority, and organizational level are highly correlated in Japan because age is a major criterion for promotion.

Americans have less equality on the job than Swedes or Israelis but more equality than the Japanese and South Americans, such as Brazilians or Argentinians. In South America, authority is centralized and controlled by top management. At the same time exposure to American values affects the local South American managers; about 80 percent of South American managers who work for U.S. subsidiaries use delegation of authority more than South American managers in local firms.

The need to avoid uncertainty is another cultural characteristic that affects communication. High uncertainty avoidance is reflected in a direct style of communication that does not leave much room for ambiguity. The communicated information consists of detailed descriptions and adherence to the formal rules and regulations. To avoid uncertainty, Israeli managers, in particular those who were born in Israel, use a direct style of straight talk, *Dugri,* this implies the concern for sincerity in the sense of being true to oneself. Israelis are most likely to tell each other directly, and very explicitly what they have in mind, even when it may lead to a confrontation.

In Israel as well as Japan, the dominant values are ones of both collectivism and high uncertainty avoidance; nevertheless, the dominant communication style in the two countries differs. An *implicit* style (e.g., avoid direct confrontation) is typical of Japan. It helps preserve group harmony and avoid conflict, but it does not reduce uncertainty. In Israel, an explicit style (e.g., engage in direct confrontation) helps to avoid uncertainty but does not fit in with the need to preserve group harmony. This inconsistency is resolved by considering the value of equality. The lack of equality in Japan compensates for the lack of openness because it clarifies the source of authority. A high level of equality in Israel encourages the use of an *explicit style* because ideas can be expressed without fear in front of superiors.

Having now looked at a number of international styles of communication, we next discuss how communication differences can be handled to avoid misunderstandings and potential conflicts.

Communication and Conflict

One key characteristic of conflict styles is whether or not the individuals involved are capable of separating issues from people. The inability to distinguish between the source and the content results in severe personal disputes.

A cultural characteristic that shapes a person's conflict style is how specific or general communicated messages are. Some cultures communicate by using concrete descriptions related to the context where the event takes place. These cultures are known to have *high-context* communication. Other cultures use abstract terms to convey messages, and the context is less relevant. These cultures are known to have *low-context* communication. Group-focused cultures are more context-oriented than self-focused cultures. Since in group-focused cultures, relationships with others are extremely important, people learn to pay attention not only to what is said but also to the context—the gestures, the orientation of the body, the objects associated with the discussion. Members of group-focused, high-context cultures are sensitive to situational features and explanations and tend to attribute others' behavior to the context, situation, or other factors external to the individual. Members of self-focused low-context cultures, in contrast, generally attribute others' behavior to characteristics internal to the individual.[5]

Individuals in low-context cultures are better able to separate the conflict issue from the person involved than those in high-context cultures. In high context cultures to disagree openly or to confront someone in public is a severe blow and an extreme insult, causing both sides to *lose face*, especially in the case of superior-subordinate communication. In group-focused, high-context cultures, face is a very important construct that is tied closely to honor, shame, and obligation. People in high-context cultures invest a lot of effort in the search for a solution, and also in the process of solving the conflict as they try to be sensitive to the other side.[6] The potential for conflict is higher between strangers in low-context cultures because these people will have less concern with saving face.

The source of authority also affects conflict resolution. For example, in France, where power differential is high, conflict is dealt with by compliance with a strong central authority. In contrast, in British companies, where power differential is lower than in France, managers use personal networks and coalitions in an attempt to solve conflicts. To avoid problems and preserve harmony, the Koreans (like the Japanese) have adopted an implicit style of communication, and they often speak ambiguously. Qualifiers like "maybe," "perhaps," "probably," and "somewhat" are frequently used by Japanese, and negative responses are often avoided in Korea. There is also an implicit understanding of the mutual overall commitment between employers and employees. In the United States and Europe, instead of implicit understanding, there are explicit agreements or contracts that specify rights and obligations. This is a big difference.

Low- and high-context cultures differ in their style of argument as well. People in the United States, for example, typically engage in fact finding that leads them to conclusions. In Russia, they look for normative codes of behavior and derive the specific solution from that code. In China, executives who have to solve conflicts between two subordinates have to meet with them separately. Mexican managers use a similar approach to solve conflicts. By contrast, American managers are most likely to get the two sides together in order to solve the conflict.

Differences between high- and low-context cultures affect communication between superiors and subordinates. In low-context cultures, superiors are more likely to criticize a subordinate directly for a poor work. In a high-context culture, superiors are very careful not to hurt the feelings of their subordinates when they have to be critical. For example, a North American supervisor might say the following: "I cannot accept this proposal as submitted. You should come up with some better ideas." A Japanese supervisor would say; "While I have the highest regard for your abilities, I would not be completely honest if I did not express my disappointment at this proposal. I must ask that you reflect further on the proposal you have submitted to me."

Group-focused and self-focused cultures thus have different patterns of communication with respect to the amount and type of communication, style of communication, and way of handling conflicts. We now turn to a detailed examination of communication in Japan (group focus, high power differential), the United States (self-focus, low power differential), France (self-focus, high power differential), and the Czech Republic (group focus, low power differential).

Communication in Japan

Japanese society is a network of groups.[7] The basic unit of the society is the father-son dyad called *ie*—namely, household. A number of households are organized around a principal household into a more complex system called *dozoku.* The urban counterpart of dozoku is the *iemoto,* basically a system of school organizations of arts and crafts that include flower arrangement, tea ceremonies, judo, painting, calligraphy, dancing, Kabuki, and so forth. *Iemoto* is a fictitious family system, with the school master regarded as its head. The master exercises supreme control, and his dyadic relationships with his students are analogous to the father-son relationship. The interlinked hierarchy of the *iemoto* is similar to the principal household-branches relationships. Disciples are joined with other disciples through their masters, who are in turn brought together through senior masters. In this way, a vast hierarchic structure is created that cuts across Japanese society at large.

The structure of patriarchal families that characterized close-knit rural communities spread to family-owned large mercantile houses in the cities. More recently, with the emergence of the industrial society, the tradition of close-knit relationships has been reflected in lifelong employment, seniority-based hierarchy, apprenticeships, training and discipline, consensus, and group decision making.

The cultural values of the group and high power differentials modify the Japanese management philosophy as expressed by the following characteristics: long-term employment; compassionate concern for employees, including personal problems; participative management and group responsibility; a bottom up decision-making system known as *ringi,* emphasis on harmony; a seniority-based reward system; an organization of both authoritative and participative management; standardized training with a view to uniform competence; job rotation with the aim of producing generalists and not confining the employee to specialized work functions.

These values are clearly reflected in the intensive corporate communication system and the channels of decision making in organizations that encompass top-down, bottom-up, horizontal, formal, and informal channels of communication.[8]

Top–Down Communication

The communication system in Japanese corporations reflects the hierarchical order and respect for seniority that exist in Japanese society at large. Japanese workers show respect to their managers even outside the work setting. However, managers are not detached from their subordinates, and there is face-to-face two way communication. Nonmanagerial levels of employees talk directly to top-level executives on work-related matters. In addition, there are occasions where the president of the company meets personally with employees for inspirational talks aimed at strengthening the organizational culture and work ethic. For example, a series of talks by President Sono Fukujiro of TDK covered both topics related directly to the work environment ("Being Creative" and "The Smart TDK Man") and themes concerning family life and society in general, ("The Ideal Couple" and "Japan's Aesthetic Culture"). Top-level executives of Japanese corporations are personally involved in selection interviews, in orientation courses for new employees, and in training programs. The training programs serve to assimilate newly hired employees into the organizational culture. At Hitachi, for example, newly hired engineers rotate through the various departments of the corporation for a period of six up to twenty four months to gain a general overview of the organization. At the same time, they become acquainted with the specific "language" of each department and are able to communicate fluently throughout the organization once they have settled down. The introductory program involves an orientation course, visits to some of the company's major factories, three months, instruction in manufacturing sections, and a twenty-month advanced program, including on-the-job training, classroom study, and voluntary self-development courses.

The importance of the training system is emphasized by its position in the organizational structure. At Hitachi, the president assumes top responsibility for education throughout the company and is supported by committees that identify the training needs of the employees. The system serves as a formal channel of communication that helps the employees adjust to their jobs and to technological changes.

Bottom–Up Communication

These channels convey the belief in group harmony and in the joint responsibility of all group members for the successful operation of the organization. It is manifested in several forms.

1. The *ringi* system: *ringi* refers to the procedure in which a document proposing a decision is passed along for approval by persons concerned. The approval is made by stamping the proposed document with an individual seal called *hanko*. A director in Nissho-Iwai, a large Japanese trading company, explains the difference

between the American and Japanese process of decision making: "Japanese decision making is the gathering of Japanese wisdom. The *ringi* system allows everyone who is likely to be involved in implementation to participate in the making of the decision. This feeling of participation is very important for the spirit of *wa.*"

This book's second author observed the way the *ringi* system operates in the Tayo-Kobe Bank in Tokyo. A customer who was interested in getting a loan for business purposes approached the manager of the loan department. The manager told him that he would examine the possibilities and conditions for the loan within a day or two. The manager then approached one of the employees of the department and asked him to prepare a proposal for a decision about the loan. This employee started to collect relevant information including the substance of conversations he had with headquarters. Next he consulted with the other members of the department before he made the proposal for the decision. The process of consultation and informal discussion is known as *nemawashi.* This process reflects the spirit of consensus and takes place before the formal proposal is presented at the official meeting. Based on the information, collected and on the advice of other members of the department, he prepared a draft proposal. The written proposal was then circulated among the department's employees. Each member approved the proposal by affixing his or her *hanko,* indicating basic acceptance. The number of *hankos* varies according to the number of people who would be affected by the decision and have to be involved in the process. When all the members of the department had approved the proposal by putting their hankos on it the decision was handed to the department manager, and he presented it to the customer. It is very rare that the manager does not accept a proposal. It may happen when he has some information that was not known to his employees.

2. Small-group activity: The process of decision making and problem solving usually takes part in teams of about eight to ten employees. The most popular form of small-group activity is the quality control circle, invented in Japan. Its purpose is to increase productivity and improve the level of quality through direct participation. The team members are volunteers and usually take a training course for the acquisition of two basic skills: data collection and analysis, and interpersonal skills necessary for group problem solving. The team leader takes a more extensive course where she or he studies how to effectively lead the team. On a constant basis the team identifies problems related to work methods, cost reduction, and quality improvement.

3. Suggestion system: In addition to the small-group activity, in most Japanese organizations the suggestion system enables individuals to put forward ideas for improvement. Each suggestion is examined within one week and ranked according to its level of contribution. Valuable suggestions are immediately implemented, and the employees who submitted the suggestions win an award. At Canon, the best proposals rate a special presidential award of an all-expense-paid, two-week tour of overseas plants. In Canon, the average number of suggestions is seventy-six per employee, and in Hitachi it is about seventy.

Middle–Up–Down Management

This form of communication bridges the gap between the visionary but abstract concepts of top management and the experience-grounded concepts originating on the shop floor. The role of the middle-level manager becomes crucial for integrating the strategic macro level with its hands-on micro counterpart. The concept of middle-up-down management was developed and implemented in Honda when top management gave a group of young designers the task of developing an entirely new car, with virtually no direction. The overall assignment from headquarters was to create something different from the existing concept. This involved two major targets—creating a popular, fuel-efficient car and designing a low-priced but not cheap model. The group then was given autonomy to lead the process, which is described by Ikujuru Nonaka in the *Sloan Management Review*.[9] The project team comprised people from the sales, engineering, and development departments, known as the SED system. The team leader, Mr. Watanabe, portrays the style of team work of the SED system: "I am always telling the team members that like in a rugby game, all of us should run together, passing the ball left and right, reaching the goal as one united body." This process leads to a high level of information sharing, as one engineer put it: "The knowledge is alive because it changes continuously.... The best way to transfer it is through human interaction."

Horizontal Communication, Formal and Informal

Lateral integration among departments is a natural process in Japanese corporations. This process is facilitated by the infrastructure of the social network, the group orientation, and the process of socialization that enables new members to learn the function and language of the various departments. Interdepartmental meetings and heterogenous teams serve the purpose of developing new products in Japan. In Pfitzer, a pharmaceutical company operating in Japan, the development of new products is discussed by representatives of the R&D center and of the manufacturing, and marketing departments. The joint discussion ensures that the proposed product has a potential market and that the cost of development and production can be offset by the market price. This procedure enables the company to avoid possible pitfalls due to lack of interdepartmental communication. Departmental and interdepartmental meetings facilitate the development of a strong organizational culture and of a smooth flow of communication across departments.

The lateral communication is accompanied by an informal system of communication. Several times a week, employees who work together meet for drinks after working hours. These meetings are basically social but encourage the exchange of information and ideas as well—sometimes as part of the small-group activity or *nemawashi* process referred to earlier. But the unique form of informal communication systems in Japanese organizations is the *Jinmyaku,* defined as the connection among people belonging to the same group or the same series of groups in the political, business, and academic worlds. *Jinmyaku* represents a hierarchical array of informal networks across groups within and outside the organization; these facilitate information sharing and provide support. *Jinmyaku,* sometimes formed around graduates of the same school, can become exclusive and out-of-bounds to outsiders. Members of *jinmyaku* help one another in obtaining promotion and support each other's decisions. Belonging to *jinmyaku* is a symbol of security and status. There is actually a saying in Japan: "Know-who is more important than know-how."

The closest analog to *jinmyaku* in Western organizations would be mentoring. The mentor helps young employees make their way in the organization. However, these mentor-employee relationships are purely dyadic, whereas in Japan *jinmyaku* is a social network. Surprisingly enough, there is no specific mention of this term in Western research literature on Japanese management, although the phenomenon was described by Peter Drucker, who felt unable to characterize it properly: "It has no name—the term *godfather* is mine, not theirs."[10]

In any event, group-focused cultures provide the natural infrastructure necessary for the development of strong communication network. In particular, the bottom-up and horizontal forms of communication are typical of these cultures. The diverse channels of communication facilitate the diffusion and creation of information necessary for the survival and renewal of organizations in the competitive era.

Communication in the United States

Unlike the Japanese firms, American corporations still struggle with the bureaucratic top-down forms of communication, preventing them from quick adaptation to the changing environment. More and more American CEOs recognize the importance of the communication network. One way U.S. firms form an informal communication system is by combining sport and business. It is not rare anymore to see CEOs power walking with top executives during lunch time. This affords them time to exercise and to have uninterrupted conversations with their chief executives. At some companies like Microsoft, sports form an integral part of the corporate culture, known as the *play hard, work hard* atmosphere.

The *virtual community* is perhaps the American version of interpersonal communication. In his book *The Virtual Community: Homesteading on the Electronic Frontier.,* Howard Rheingold describes this community. In their living rooms people participate in spirited conversations by tapping on their computer keyboards and powering up their modems. The virtual community consists of a group of people who probably have not met face to face but who enjoy spending time together in cyberspace. They debate politics, do business, or just flirt and play games. The members of the virtual community are not just interested in the information available on the Internet. Rather, they are longing to form relationships with their farflung neighbors in the global village.

Although the Western self-focused values do not cultivate a person-to-person communication as developed in Japan, Western cultures can take advantage of the new technological developments that facilitate corporate communication. An interesting case of adjusting a group decision-making process to fit a self-focused culture has been implemented in a number of American companies. This method is known as groupware, and it allows for a group of people to participate indecision making via the keyboard and the computer screen.

All participants communicate at once by typing in their ideas and comments, sending them simultaneously to the computer screens of all other participants and at the same time, receiving comments from all other participants. This form of communication saves a significant amount of time, up to 90 percent, and yet allows all participants to share ideas and to influence the decision-making process. IBM and Boeing were among the first companies to install the communication technology for groupware. At Dell Computer, the use of groupware went so well that the company has started using it for any type of project that requires groups of people to work together, like product planning and developing marketing strategies. For example, Dell used the system to name a new product. A group of marketing managers met for two hours, proposed and rated seventy-five names, and reduced them to five finalists. It would have taken two months to get to that point the old way. Companies that implemented the Groupware system reported a significant improvement in the quality and productivity of meetings. Groups were able to reach a genuine consensus, and their members became more committed to decisions than they would have been with conventional methods. The new groupware tools are so powerful that they virtually compel companies to reengineer themselves. Groupware spreads power by giving workers well below the top of the organizational pyramid access to information previously unavailable or restricted to upper-level management. Companies who use groupware become less concerned with the question of who needs to know what. Instead managers simply forward their memos to the appropriate bulletin board, and anyone who needs to know about a subject checks there and finds it.

Hundreds of American companies, including Price Waterhouse, Compac Computer, Chase Manhattan, General Motors, Reebok, and Texaco, have also logged on to Lotus Notes software for groups. Meeting software allows participants in face-to-face or video conference gathering to "talk" simultaneously by typing on PC keyboards. Because people read faster than they speak and don't have to wait for others to finish talking, the software can dramatically speed progress toward consensus. It also helps ensure that everyone gets a chance to take part. Networking is making computers more and more interpersonal. It helps bridge conceptual gaps between employees while giving them power they never had previously.

The use of E-mail is another prevalent form of electronic communication of American companies. A growing number of employees start their work day by checking messages on their computers; they subscribe to electronic bulletin boards that furnish information and post questions for others. Moreover the use of electronic mail is not exclusive to big corporations. More and more individuals subscribe to electronic-mail networks. Such a communication network is WELL (Whole Earth 'Lectronic Link) which began in 1985 as an experiment to let ordinary people determine how to use new tools for group communication. The network has become the ultimate social leveler: black and white, old and young, male and female, members enter conversations about everything from birth control to childbearing. The estimate is that in two years there will be more network users than there are people living in California.

Communication in France

Although advanced in technology and progressive French organizations are guided by two general principles—a strong emphasis on hierarchy and bureaucracy as well as a top-down style of communication. Unlike American and Japanese firms, French corporations still employ a bureaucratic, top-down form of communication that inhibits quick adaptation to the changing environment. In fact, this bureaucracy has its origins in the French government system, which dates back hundreds of years. The reliance on centralization and hierarchy reflects the cultural orientation of France, a strong self-focus combined with a high power differential. Let us take, for example, the strikes led by farmers, protesting changes in agriculture laws because of European Union membership. The civil disobedience of the farmers, who threw their produce down in front of the French parliament reflects the high power differentials and the general attitude that the aristocrats and politicians are fundamentally different than the proletariat, or common workers. This split between social classes is present in French companies as well and is one of the reasons that communication relies on formal channels, formal documentation, and formal protocols.

Another example can be found at Crédit Lyonnaise, a state-owned French bank, which recently has received a rescue package from the government for nearly $3.5 billion (FFr 20 billion). A number of the problems of this bank have been attributed to poor management and communication and to an inability to respond to the changing financial markets in the European Union. The bank's strong central authority—in which information concerning markets and key investment opportunities must travel through an extensive hierarchy—means that response times are sluggish and slow. However, through the practice of moving information from one level to the next to the next, slows things down, it does offer an advantage: messages are seen by everyone who might be affected, and they are usually kept clear and accurate. For an expatriate manager, this process means that communication in a French company involves patience and adherence to standard channels. Crossing over the normal channels in order to get things done quickly is likely to be met with hesitation and resistance.

Communication in the Czech Republic

In our final example, we glimpse the nature of communication the Czech Republic, a country undergoing many significant transitions as a result of the Velvet Revolution of 1989.[12] The Czech Republic is a rapidly emerging capitalist system with a strong tradition of socialism and communism. Formerly part of Czechoslovakia, the republic was part of the general alliance of communist countries created by the former Soviet Union. After the Velvet Revolution the country split itself into two semiautonomous states, Czech Republic and Slovakia, and created separate legislatures. While the pace of capitalist reform in the Czech Republic is quite high, management practices, and organizational and societal culture reflect a strong orientation toward group identification and a low power differential. An assessment by two Czech scientists found that a sample of university students endorsed a number of values, including living in a happy family, helping those close themselves, having good friendships, and living and working in peace. These dominant values reflect a general collective orientation (group loyalty and team action) and a rejection of a traditional emphasis on political involvement (with the value of being politically active as the lowest ranked by four separate Czech groups, including first- and fourth- year university students, Prague youths, and *Ceske Budejovice* citizens). Some recent evidence, however, suggests that this team orientation may be changing as well for senior-level management. A recent poll of twenty senior Czech managers conducted by Eschenbach on behalf of the management consulting group of Roland, Berger, and Partner showed that they more strongly endorsed individualistic work values (for themselves) than did similar groups of managers from Slovakia and Austria.[12]

Although a number of Czech state-owned companies have been fully or partly privatized, evidence suggests that such reforms are still being met with some degree of skepticism. For instance, a recent strike in the fall of 1994 of over eight thousand workers from the Skoda automobile plant (one of the single largest state-owned companies in the republic) reflected a growing fear among employees that the reforms might be taking place at the cost of economic sovereignty. In this instance, Skoda employees were expressing concern over the privatization of Skoda in an alliance with Volkswagen.

The way employees communicate in the Czech Republic can be illustrated by looking at the company that is privatizing Skoda. This company is involved in a wide range of manufacturing activities—heavy and light manufacturing, agriculture, and construction. It retains a strong hierarchical form based on the former communist system, and chains-of-command are easily observed in formal organizational charts. These suggest that the Czech Republic has many of the features of the French bureaucratic system. However, the inefficiency of this large company has led many Czech employees to rely on informal ways of getting work done.

In talking with a number of managing directors from large Czech companies, we have heard that many of them reduce the time it takes to communicate ideas and information by using informal channels, friendships, and key informants to communicate. For instance, a finance manager had learned about a new way of assessing the quality of engine housing. Rather than using the formal chain-of-command in the company, he contacted a family friend in production and met with him over drinks and dinner. The manager in production did not have enough authority to implement a manufacturing change, so he called a friend who was several organizational levels above himself in production. After relaying the suggestions to his friend, the chief manager of production got his management team together and convinced them about the merits of the idea. The net result was that the finance manager's idea was implemented for a substantial cost savings for the company.

This idea adoption reflects the unique nature of Czech corporate communicadon; There is a formally recognized path for communication and decision making that is often passed by. The formal channels do not provide managers with big incentives, and the risks of failure are often quite obvious. Why then would a Czech manager initiate a change or improvement? The connections among friends (reflected by the strong group focus) means that one person can help out others by passing along valuable information. A Czech manager who communicates a job improvement to a friend will both help that person gain company credit and establish a debt that she or he will repay at some future point. Thus the communication seen in the Czech Republic is based on favors, friendship, and exchanges. Jone Pearce and Imre Brazcynski describe a similar pattern in their studies of Hungarian managers.[13] People don't hesitate to violate the formal chain-of-command because of their low, cultural power differential, and they use social connections to exchange ideas.

Summary

Culture influences the amount, style, and nature of communication in companies across the globe. The level of person-to-person communication is higher in group-focused than in self-focused cultures. In turn, the communication system facilitates the sharing of values, leading to the formation of tight-knit cultures. For instance, the Japanese patterns of communication within and between organizations correspond to the cultural values of the society: they help preserve group consensus through participation in decision making and group harmony through the processes of conflict resolution. We summarize our discussion in Table 4.1.

Interorganization communication networks strengthen the sharing of culture across a nation. The Japanese market can be viewed as consisting of circles from the inner level of the work group, through the level of organizational units, corporations at large, *keiretsu* (collections of related companies), and the Japanese society at large. The communication network serves as the glue that holds Japanese society together, and it interlinks the Japanese corporations with the greater society. The company book of Hitachi, *Hitachi and Modern Japan,* symbolically represents the ties between the corporations and society. The collective identity of the individual employee is developed through interactions with others. Similarly, Japanese corporate identity acquires its meaning in relation to society.

American corporations, unlike Japanese firms, are anchored in an self-focused culture that does not provide the supportive infrastructure for intense communication. Their way to deal with the necessity to enhance communication has been the adoption of electronic communication. This facilitates information flow while avoiding face-to-face communication and personal contact. Electronic communication does not violate privacy, does not create mutual commitment, and is not sensitive to individual differences in age, gender, or race. This channel of communication is suitable for low-context, self-focused culture. Even so, cultural bias can still cause misunderstanding. For example, the E-mail correspondence

Table 4.1

Summary of Effective Communication in Various Cultures

	Low Power Differential	High Power Differential
Self-focused	There is open flow with each person responsible for knowing enough to remain independent. People communicate up, down, and laterally within their functional units and businesses. Electronic mail, computer messaging, and teleconferencing are substitutes for person-to-person contact. At a company level, units do not share information even when a vertically superior company (e.g., parent headquarters of a subsidiary) instructs them to do so. Exchange is kept short and only gives the essential information requested. Examples: United States, New Zealand, Finland	There are downward communication channels with an emphasis on keeping people independent. Goals and directives come from above through a chain-of-command to individuals and not groups. Communication is frank, but but deference is paid to people in superior positions. At a company level, units do not share much information unless they are told to by vertically superior companies. Examples: South Africa, Italy, Spain
Group-focused	There is group-focused open flow to, from, and within groups or teams. People will communicate with a group member knowing that the entire group will receive the information from that person. People in a close-knit group communicate frankly with one another and share all information. At a company level, communication occurs across businesses having related organizational members such as shared board members or managing directors. Examples: Jamaica, Argentina, Israel	There is strong emphasis on downward communication flow. Impersonal communication methods like E-mail or written memos are used to keep the differences between a supervisor and subordinate clear. Upward communication emphasizes positive aspects of work and avoids presenting "bad news" that might embarrass a person's superior. At a company level, communication occurs in a vertical fashion such as the Japanese keiretsu. Examples: South Korea, Mexico, Singapore, Saudi Arabia, Japan

between Israelis and Americans of the same multinational company reveals that the Israelis feel free to disagree and criticize their counterparts. Moreover, they ask personal questions that are not directly work related. The Americans, by contrast, avoid criticism, are likely to be offended, and feel uncomfortable answering personal questions. Their response is likely to be interpreted by the Israelis as unfriendly.

Cultural differences in communication thus have a direct effect on any activity that requires joint efforts across nations. Multinational and transnational managers have to be familiar with the self-knowledge and cultures, as well as the communication styles, of their counterparts and must have a shared understanding of how to communicate. In the next chapter, we describe the importance of self-knowledge and culture as a basis for developing successful teams and teamwork. With the challenge of the information explosion facing competitive companies throughout the world, teams of employees must work together in order to work effectively.

5

Motivating Employees in Different Cultures

Modern organizations attempt to select the most talented, capable, and knowledgeable people available. Organizations compete heavily for high-caliber employees. In exchange for offering an attractive employment package, they expect that these employees will work to the full extent of their abilities and exert all their effort and mental resources in their workplace. Very often this assumption is proven wrong, and employees fail to reach their potential. Although they may have the talent, they may lack motivation and drive. Motivated employees have three major characteristics: they have a sense of direction; they know where they want to go and what they want to accomplish. They have a willingness to try hard and to exert effort. Finally, they do not give up even when they face obstacles that thwart goal achievement. In contrast, those who are not motivated lack commitment to their work and don't pay attention to what is required of them. As a result, they do not gain a sense of accomplishment, do not receive rewards and recognition, and become unsatisfied and withdrawn.

For several decades, the Roper Organization in New York City has been polling about 1,200 employees every few years and has found job satisfaction in America to be at its lowest level during the early 1990s. In its survey of one thousand large corporations, the Hay Group found that the percentage of middle managers expressing favorable attitudes toward their companies dropped from 65 percent in 1987 to 55 percent in 1990. Only 43 percent thought that companies treated them with respect as individuals, and only 35 percent thought that top management listened to their problems and complaints.[1] Clearly, motivating employees is a critical issue in the modern workplace. The purpose of this chapter is twofold. First, we will identify what leads employees either to become highly motivated or to lose their motivation. Second, we will explore how managers around the world can increase their employees' motivation by examining cultural influences on reward methods, decision-making and goal-setting techniques, and job and organizational design systems.

What Creates Human Motivation?

All human beings are motivated to develop a positive self-knowledge and a sense of self-worth and well-being. More specifically employees are motivated to fulfill the three basic self-motives described earlier: self-enhancement, self-growth, and self-consistency. Therefore effective managers should learn to identify the basic self-motives of their employees and the cultural values that shape their self-worth and well-being. In particular, managers should assess whether the culture is self-focused or group-focused and whether the power differential in the society is high or low. Further they need to learn to discern whether their own managerial approach creates opportunities for their employees to satisfy their self-motives. Managers should strive to create a work environment that provides employees with opportunities to feel good about themselves, to experience a sense of competence and control, and to behave in a manner consistent with their values, norms, and beliefs. By doing so, effective managers harness employees' motivation to the benefit of their companies.

In Chapter 2 we offered a technique and tools for assessing self-motives and cultural values. In this chapter, we will point out the motivational techniques that most effectively satisfy employees' self-motives in different cultures. One of the challenges that managers face is how to link employee motivation to organizational goals, to tie the attainment of organizational goals to a sense of self-worth and well-being. For example, high-tech companies such as Intel and Microsoft recognize that their professional employees are motivated to develop their skills and that they enjoy opportunities to practice their knowledge by taking responsibility and making decisions. From the company's perspective, professional employees are important assets; by delegating more responsibility to them and providing ways for them to use and expand their skills, the company maximizes its human resource potential.

A motivating reward system makes the distribution of rewards contingent upon employees, behavior and output and signals employees whether to persist in their behavior or to change it. In-effective managers fail to provide the rewards that are directly related to desired employee behavior and outcomes. For example, though some managers invest a great deal of time and effort defining what rewards to use, they do not define clearly the type of activities or the performance that should be rewarded. In other words, in the absence of precise performance standards, employees do not know what exactly is expected from them in order to gain rewards. Others make the opposite mistake. They clearly define the goals that are important to the company but do not differentiate between high and low performers in meting out rewards. In either case, managers have failed to create a link between employee performance and rewards, a failure leading to a lack of motivation and poor performance. This problem is seen mainly in self-focused cultures, where employees use their personal standards to evaluate their

Table 5.1

Common Problems with Reward Systems and Potential Solutions

	Poorly implemented	Properly implemented

Performance standard	Poorly defined
	Not communicated
	Nonspecific
	Targeted at inappropriate
	    organization level
		Clearly defined
		Clearly communicated
		Precise standards
		Targeted at appropriate
		    organization level

Performance measurements	Not measured
	Vague perceptions
	Irregular measurement
	Measured at inappropriate
	    organization level
		Specific behavior(s)
		Quantifiable output
		Regularly measured
		Targeted at appropriate
		    organization level

Rewards	Not allocated in accord with
	    performance level
	Not tailored to meet individual
	    needs and preferences.
	Not allocated in accord with
	    cultural values
		Tailored to individual
		    motives and preferences
		Distributed according to
		    successful attainment of
		    performance criteria
		Allocated in accord
		    with cultural values

self-worth and well-being. Employees in highly egalitarian, group-focused cultures, also require defined organizational objectives, but they are rewarded by working as part of a team; they feel good about themselves when their team excels and receives recognition and seek rewards that are shared equally by the team members. Table 5.1 summarizes common mistakes made in the implementation of reward systems and provides a suggested technique to link rewards to performance.

Effective motivational approaches require that managers define the performance criteria, the type of rewards, and the formula that ties rewards to behavior. To do so, managers must learn what kind of rewards are valued by their employees, and what is the source of evaluation used by the employees. Figure 5.1 presents a model specifying how to motivate employees by creating jobs that simultaneously fulfill their self-motives as well as organizational goals. According to this model, cultural values, individual motives, and organizational demands influence the shaping of the work environment and the job requirements. Employee behavior is defined and directed by these requirements, which should be explicitly stated by the organization but which may change as organizations change their goals. With properly designed and implemented reward systems, employee behaviors will lead to outcomes that benefit both the organization and individual employees.

How Motivational Approaches Vary Across Cultures

Motivational techniques that are highly valued according to cultural standards of employees are most likely to facilitate this sense of accomplishment. Logically motivational techniques that are at odds with prevailing cultural values are unlikely to be effective. Since cultures differ in the values they endorse, people may interpret the same motivational techniques quite differently. In the following section, we explore the effectiveness of three major motivational techniques using a cultural approach: rewards for employees, methods for decision making and goal setting, and the design of jobs and organizations. These will be discussed in relation to the four major types of cultures: group focus/low power differential, group focus/high power differential, self-focus/low power differential, and self-focus/high power differential. Although our illustrations are drawn from a limited set of countries, they do represent each of the four major types of cultures, and the general principles

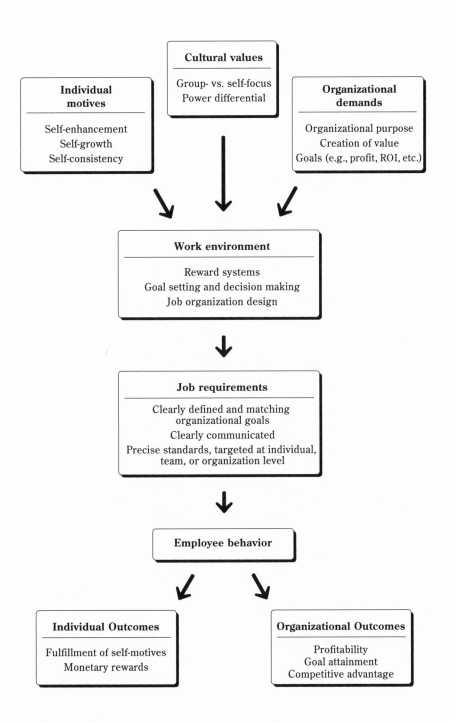

Figure 5.1 *Motivating employees by creating jobs that fulfill both self-motives and organizational goals*

Table 5.2

*Strategies for Motivational Techniques According to Cultural
Dimensions of Focus and Power Differentials*

	Low power differential	High power differential
Self-focus		
Rewards	*The rule of equity* Individual incentives, profit sharing, gain sharing *The rule of equality* low salary differential welfare and fringe benefits based on demographics (e.g., family size, disability)	*The rule of equity* Individual incentives, high salary differential
Decision Making	Delegation of authority, individual decision making	Top-down, centralized
Goal-setting	Personal involvement in goal setting	Assigned individual goals
Job Design	Enrichment of individual jobs	Individual jobs in a hierarchy of authority and responsibility
Examples	*Equity:* Australia, Canada, Britain, United States. *Equality:* the Netherlands, New Zealand	*Equity:* Belgium, France, Italy, Spain, South Africa
Group-focus		
Rewards	*The rule of equality or needs* Equally distributed organization-based rewards, equally distributed employee stock ownership plans	*The rule of equity or needs* group-based rewards, Unequally distributed organiza tion-based rewards un- equally distributed employee stock ownership plans
Decision Making	Delegation of authority, Group participation	Top-down, Centralized decision-making
Goal-setting	Group goal setting	Assigned group goals
Job Design	Autonomous work groups, Self-managed team, quality circles	Team work controlled by top management teams, quality circles
Examples	*Equality and needs:* Israel, Costa Rica, Norway, Finland, Denmark, Sweden, Uruguay, Venezuela *Needs:* India	*Equity:* Japan, Korea, Singapore, Philippines, Brazil, Jamaica

we discuss can be applied virtually anywhere. The information in Table 5.2 can help you decide which motivational techniques will be most effective for companies in each of the four types of cultures.

Rewarding Employees

There are two central cultural values that shape both employee evaluation of reward systems and the effectiveness of motivational techniques: group versus individually focused cultures and the cultural power differential. In an individually focused culture, people use independent, personal standards to assess the impact of motivational techniques on their sense of self-worth and well-being, whereas in a group-focused culture, interdependent, group-based standards are used. The second cultural characteristic, the power differential, reflects the level of inequality in societies, or the distance between different levels in organizational hierarchies. Employees in societies with high levels of inequality (a high power differential) pay strong respect to their superiors and avoid criticizing them. There are often large discrepancies in the compensation and quality of working life of managers and nonmanagers and in the managerial levels of the organization. In addition status symbols often differentiate superiors and subordinates.

Reward systems across cultures are created under the guiding influence of three different allocation principles. These are the principle of *equity* (to each according to contribution), the principle of *equality* (to each equally), and the principle of *need* (to each according to need). These principles are the result of preferences for individualism or for collectivism, for egalitarianism or for high power differential.

The equity principle is commonly used in individualistic cultures with either a low or high power differential—for instance, the United States, Canada, and Britain on the low side and Italy, France, and South Africa on the high side. In these countries, individual accomplishment and recognition are emphasized over group harmony and teamwork. Though dominant in these types of cultures, the principle of equity is only one of three methods used to allocate rewards in the global market. The equality principle is much more common in group-focused cultures with low power differential like Israel, Costa Rica, and Finland. Equality reflects an emphasis on encouraging employees to work together as equals and a complementary managerial style focusing on coordination rather than creation of competition for rewards.

Finally, the need principle is found in developing countries like Pakistan. This principle prevails in societies with shortages of fundamental necessities—food and housing, for example. The need principle assumes that there is a basic level of rewards for everyone, and that satisfaction of this level takes priority over individual accomplishment or group harmony.

Early management thought in the United States (circa 1911), pioneered by Frederick Taylor, advocated the philosophy of compensation based on an individual's performance and the establishment of individual piece-rate plans. This principle of equity is at the foundation of individual incentive plans extensively implemented in the United States. Typically these are based on individual performance evaluations that determine the level of compensation for a particular employee. According to this system, two employees who have the same job can get different levels of compensation when one receives a better performance evaluation. Evaluations can be determined either objectively (e.g., number of units produced or the customers served) or subjectively (e.g., supervisor evaluations). Individual incentive plans based on personal merit are consistent with the individualistic values of American culture and are highly accepted by both employees and management.

In the United States, rewards distributed on the basis of individual merit take various forms, such as a personal bonus, profit sharing, and stock options. The level of inequality there is increasing: the pay gap between CEOs and others is continually widening. A report in *Business Week* shows that in 1990, even as profits declined 7 percent, the average chief executive's total pay climbed to $1,952,806.[2] Between 1980 and 1990, employees received a 53 percent increase in pay, whereas corporate profit increased by 78 percent, and CEO compensation by 212 percent. A more recent report demonstrates that the gap increased from 1990 to 1992. The average annual compensation was $24,411 for rank-and-file employees, $34,098 for teachers, $58,240 for engineers, and $3,842,247 for CEOs.[3]

Reward principles are quite different in other cultures, of course. As an example, managers in China use the equality principle more often in allocating rewards.[4] This orientation can be explained by China's group-focused values. Furthermore, managers are more likely to operate under prevailing cultural values in the presence of others and particularly when they are allocating rewards to members of their own group.

In addition, using the principles of equity versus equality depends on the purpose at hand. For instance, people tend to use the principle of equity more in competitive work environments than when working with neighbors.[5] In the latter case, people seem to rely on equality for maintaining friendships. This situational difference (work versus home neighborhood) is found both in South Korea (a group-focused culture) and in the United States (a self-focused culture). Overall, however, Koreans, unlike Americans, are more favorable to managers who use the equality principle than those who use the equity principle.

The use of equity and equality principles differs not only between the United States and Pacific Rim but also between the United States and Europe, as well as among different European countries. For example. A "payment by results" approach, similar to the equity principle and consistent with individualistic values, is most highly implemented in Britain and Ireland (40–45 percent of all salaried employees) but is not often used in the Netherlands (only 19 percent of all salaried employees).[6] These cultures differ in their degree of collectivism, with the Netherlands displaying a more collective or group-focused culture.

The type of reward schemes that emerge in each country thus accords with prevailing cultural characteristics. Attempts to transfer a reward system from one culture to another can result in a mismatch, and dissonant systems are likely to be ineffective and rejected. The following case, a public utility company in Israel, exemplifies the difficulties of using mismatched reward systems. Dr. Uri Gloskinus, a private organizational development consultant, implemented an MBO (management by objectives) program in the National Water Company of Israel. This program consisted of setting individual performance goals aimed at cost reduction; coupled with individual performance appraisals, these served as the criterion for payment by results. Each area manager in the company was responsible for employee performance appraisals, as well as for allocating rewards based on individual performance. Goal setting was very effective and resulted in a significant energy cost reduction. However, mixed opinions were expressed by employees, who viewed the appraisal procedure as very threatening. In fact, the local union, which cited a couple of incidents in which appraisals may have been conducted inappropriately, used these cases to demand the halt of the written evaluations. The opposition to the appraisals occurred even though most were quite positive, and only a few were really negative. The bonus system, although it increased the net income of employees, was opposed by 40 percent of them. Most comments suggested rewarding teams rather than individuals to improve the bonus system.

The negative responses to this differential performance appraisal and reward scheme can only be understood fully by interpreting them in terms of the dominant values of the company: it is in the public sector, employees are unionized, and employees have lifetime employment. Salary and compensation have always been distributed according to equality principle, and promotion is determined primarily by seniority. The company's organizational culture reflects the national Israeli values of collectivism and egalitarianism. The individual performance appraisal system and the differential reward system, originally designed for an individualistic culture, were incongruent with Israeli cultural values. Employees in group-focused and egalitarian cultures develop their sense of self-worth and well-being through their relationships with others; these can be threatened by an individual performance appraisal that fosters independence and competition.

Northern European countries are also more group-centered and egalitarian than the Australia, Britain, and the United States. For example, the Swedish education system, unlike the American one discourages competition in favor of cooperation; it fosters teamwork and solidarity rather than individual achievement. The Swedes, unlike Americans, give first preference to the equality principle, followed by needs, and finally by equity. The strong emphasis on group membership influences promotion decisions in Sweden. Employees with a high ability to cooperate are more likely to be promoted to top managerial levels than others. Japan is another culture where cooperation is considered to be an important factor in promotion decisions.

A comparison of India and the United States shows that Indians, more than Americans, use the principle of need as the basis for reward allocation. People in that nation are more sensitive to the requirements of others, and these are more visible in India than in other countries. Indians seem to be less sensitive to the concept of merit since social status in their society is determined by family rather than by individual achievement alone.

The cases just described demonstrate that cultural values (preferences for a group versus self-focus, and egalitarianism versus a high power differential) clearly affect the way that managers reward employees. In individualistic cultures like Canada and the United States, the equity principle tends to drive the allocation of rewards. When need or equality principles are used, they take the form of a welfare system using individual-based criteria: a person's family size, personal disability, and so forth. In other words, even when a principle other than the equity principle is used, it is often employed in an equity fashion. This situation also holds true in organizations. For example, some companies that use teamwork, such as IBM and Xerox, reward teams based on their varying accomplishments. This approach fosters competition among teams even though everyone in a given team may get an equal reward. Some U.S. companies go further by giving individual rewards within a team as well as team rewards.

Individually based performance pay conflicts with teamwork because it creates competition between team members and often does not provide incentives for cooperation. American companies that encourage teamwork have been looking for alternatives to individual incentives. In their book *Employee Involvement and Total Quality Management,* Lawler, Mohrman, and Ledford report percentages of Fortune 1,000 corporations using various performance-based rewards in 1987 and 1990. They found that 11 percent of the companies employed individual incentives in 1987, compared with 20 percent in 1990; team incentives were used by 12 percent of the companies in 1990, and no data were available for 1987. Profit-sharing plans increased slightly, from 34 percent to 37 percent; use of gain-sharing plans remained steady at 3 percent; and employee stock ownership plans increased very slightly, from 48 percent to 49 percent. Thus it seems that American companies use employee stock ownership plans more than any other form of rewards, although they are still divided unequally among the employees and are based on their organizational position and performance evaluation.

The challenge to management is to develop an appropriate reward scheme that fits with cultural norms and does not thwart teamwork and employee motivation.

Making Decisions and Setting Goals

Decision making and goal setting can be undertaken by individuals or teams in a participative or nonparticipative form. Participation in goal setting and decision making was first employed in the United States by German-born social psychologist Kurt Lewin in order to help people overcome resistance to change. He believed that employees who participate in the process of decision making are more highly motivated to support an eventual decision for three reasons. First, they are personally involved, and this involvement gives them a sense of control over decisions that affect them and thereby make them more committed to the outcome. Second, employees learn and gain information as part of the decision-making process, therefore they make better decisions and have a better understanding of what has to be done. (This point is very important in a competitive world where ideas and the contributions of every employee are needed to help companies remain competitive. A special report on how to compete in the global economy published in *Business Week* calls on managers to "put aside dictatorial ways, give employees a voice in their jobs, and—most importantly—enable workers to develop new skills throughout their careers.")[7] Third, group participation creates a dynamic process that puts pressure on individual members to keep to the group decision, especially when that is made publicly.

Participation as a concept is not value free. From a political perspective, it increases workers' control over the workplace and enforces the belief that participatory democracy at work is a social value in itself. This value is more highly institutionalized in Europe than in the United States. In some European countries, such as Germany, compulsory employee participation in decision making is dictated by legislation. In the United States, participation is advocated but voluntarily adopted. The tendency for employees to comply with the goals given to them by managers is to some extent a cultural characteristic. In cultures with a high power differential, employees are more likely to comply with goals assigned by their superiors than in cultures with a low power differential.

As noted previously, France represents a self-focused, high power differential culture with a long tradition of centralization, hierarchical rigidity, individual respect for authority, and elitism. Power in French companies resides with the Président-Directeur-Générale (PDG). He or she is the one *who* decides, executes, and controls company policy. In addition, top-level executives in France believe that they should make all the critical decisions and that they should check the decisions made by others.[8] Employees in French companies respect their superiors, trust them, and expect them to make the important decisions and to solve problems. Given this, French employees are likely to accept the directions and decisions made by superiors, a situation making participation less highly valued.

Based on our discussion here, an important question arises: how much participation should be used in the process of setting goals and making decisions that affect their attainment? Some insight to the answer can be found in the following cases. The first illustrates the importance of who sets the goals for employees. Two tire manufacturing companies (one in the United States, the other in Britain) tested the effectiveness of two sources of goal setting.[9] The first one involved having managers set goals for their employees. In the second, shop stewards, rather than managers, set the objectives. The second technique produced greater increases in employee performance in Britain but not in the United States. In Britain, a goal program sponsored by shop stewards is more consistent with the labor relations system than a manager-sponsored program. Furthermore, the opportunity to influence decision-making process through representatives strengthened the employees' sense of self-worth. Although both the United States and Britain are cultures with high self-focus and low power differential, the latter is more collectivistic than the United States. Therefore decisions made by the shop stewards, who are closer to the employees than upper-level managers, are more acceptable.

While this example highlights the need to consider the impact of cultural differences when deciding who should set goals, the second case more directly explores the role of participation in goal setting. Three methods to set work goals (i.e., group participation, participation by representatives, and no participation) were examined in the United States and Israel.[10] As we have already seen, Israelis show a strong preference for working in groups and making joint decisions. Employee participation programs are institutionalized in the labor relations system, taking the form of work councils and employee representation. The highest level of participation is implemented in the kibbutz sector, where ultimate decision-making power resides with the general assembly of all the kibbutz members.

A comparison of the three methods of setting work goals in Israel and the United States showed that when goal difficulty was low, participative methods were no better than assigned goals (no participation) in both cultures. There were no differences in the level of either commitment or performance, and all employees were able to attain their work goals. When goal difficulty was high, differences between the cultures and among the motivational techniques became apparent. Employees who participated in setting objectives were more committed to them than workers who did not (in both Israel and the United States). At the same time, the performance level of American employees was not greatly affected by participation; those who did not take part in goal setting performed nearly as well as those who did. In contrast, Israeli employees who did not participate performed much worse than Israelis who played a role in the process. This finding suggests that the differences between the two countries are not linked so much to the effects of participation as to the greater group-focused culture of the Israelis.

Cultural diversity also occurs among subcultures within a single country. For example, Israel has three industrial sectors that vary with respect to the ideology of participation: the private sector, which is guided by utilitarian goals with no explicit policy of employee participation; Histadrut (the federation of most unions in Israel), which is guided by the values of collectivism and implements participation in the form of work councils and employee representation in management; and the kibbutz sector, with its emphasis on group rather than individual welfare and on egalitarian rather than utilitarian approaches to profit sharing. The three sectors create three very different work environments.

When the three methods of setting work goals (group participation, participation by representatives, and no participation) were implemented in the three sectors, each was most effective in one of the three sectors: group participation was most effective in the kibbutz sector; participation by representatives was most successful in the Histadrut sector; and nonparticipation worked best in the private sector.[11] Once again, direct group participation was found to be most effective in a highly egalitarian, collectivistic culture.

Companies within a single country may differ in their organizational cultures as well. For example, Wal-Mart, the second-ranked retail company among the Fortune 500 companies, nurtures an organizational culture that supports team spirit and a sense of egalitarianism among its 364,000 employees.[12] The late Sam Walton, founder of Wal-Mart, was known to drive a pick-up truck in order to live "a little more like real folks." Wal-Mart's culture supports working hard and having a good time. According to Walton, it's a sort of "whistle while you work" philosophy. Employees are told that if they have an important business problem, they should bring it out in the open so that others can help them try to solve it. Some of the management practices in Wal-Mart include sharing profits, treating work associates as partners, appreciating what work associates do for the business and celebrating their successes, and pushing responsibility and authority down to the lower echelons of the organization.

Of course, participation in management can be implemented within particular departments as well as entire organizations. For example, the personnel manager of a utility company in the United States decided to conduct performance appraisal interviews as part of the organization's MBO program. During the interviews, employees were asked to set goals jointly for the coming year and to discuss criteria for goal attainment. The personnel manager noticed that the appraisal interviews were not equally effective across departments. In some, joint discussions enhanced the level of motivation and performance. In others, they created a threatening atmosphere because employees did not have the self-confidence to make decisions by themselves; the process subsequently decreased motivation and performance. A detailed exploration of departmental differences revealed that the managerial culture in some departments was participative and so the new performance appraisal approach was a success. However, the participative appraisal interviews were not well received by employees who were used to an authoritarian style and had no training in taking an active role in decision making.

A similar finding is true for other participative techniques. Take, for instance, the implementation of quality circles in countries such as Israel. Quality circles have been successful in industrial plants when other forms of employee participation, such as labor-management councils already existed but were unsuccessful in industrial plants with a predominantly authoritative managerial style. When motivational techniques are inconsistent with the organizational or departmental culture, they are likely to violate the employee's internal motive of self-consistency.

Perhaps the most popular example of participative management today is that practiced in Japan. Employee participation takes the form of small-group activities, quality circles, suggestion systems, and the ringi system. We noted earlier that decisions in Japan are reached by group consensus; all employees who are affected take part in the decision-making process. By doing so, they become committed to the decision gain knowledge and understanding necessary to implement it. Although the process itself is time consuming, once a decision is made, its implementation is immediate and smooth. Participative management in Japan corresponds to the collectivistic values emphasizing team work, group harmony, and consensus. It also fits with the strong emphasis on friendships and family relationships prevalent in Japanese culture.

Thus we see that cultural values shape people's reactions to various types of decision making and goal setting. These can be undertaken by individuals or teams. In low power differential cultures like Norway or Sweden, decision making is more likely to be participative than in high power differential cultures. When a culture has a low power differential and is individualistic like the

United States, individual employees have a voice and get involved in decision making. In group-centered and low power differential cultures like Mainland China or Israel, there is more group decision making and group goal setting than in individualistic cultures.

Designing Jobs and Organizations

Jobs can be designed in many different ways. Obviously it is crucial to balance the need for effective and efficient job performance with the need to make work personally rewarding and satisfying in order to motivate job holders. In the early 1980s, two U.S. psychologists who study motivation, Richard Hackman and Greg Oldham, were able to identify five core job characteristics that have the potential to enrich jobs in ways that increase a job's ability to meet individual self-motives and thereby increase employee motivation.[13]

The first characteristic is known as *skill variety,* which allows a person to use a large variety of skills. This opportunity increases job interest and the feeling of competence and personal growth. *Task identity,* the second characteristic, is experienced when employees identify the piece of work they do as distinct and separate from other pieces in the production process. For example, a low sense of identity may occur on an assembly line. If performing one operation in an extended manufacturing process along with many other employees, a worker may be unable to understand how his or her job fits into the big picture. *Task significance,* the third characteristic, assesses the extent to which an employee thinks that the job has an impact on the lives of others. Skill variety, task identity, and task significance make work more meaningful. Autonomy at work is the fourth job characteristic that enhances individual self-worth. *Autonomy* creates a sense of self-control over work outcomes and also personal responsibility. The fifth job characteristic is *feedback* on performance, or knowledge of results. Feedback gives an employee a sense of competence and directs a person to take corrective steps in the direction of improvement. Jobs designed to increase these five characteristics are known as *enriched* jobs. Job enrichment coincides with the new managerial philosophy of quality improvement and customer satisfaction.

The job enrichment approach is designed for individual employees, not for teams. Its advocates believe that it is safer to design enriched jobs for the individual than for the group because of the added complications of group dynamics. However, one difficulty associated with enriching group activities may stem from a lack of knowledge and experience on the part of American managers in managing teams and in dealing with the interpersonal aspects of teamwork. This problem may be less prevalent in collectivistic and group-oriented societies such as Japan, Sweden, and Israel.

The most modern approach to job design in the United States is known as reengineering—the search for and implementation of significant changes in business practices to achieve breakthrough results. Reengineering is driven by the new managerial approach of quality improvement that focuses on the system rather than the individual, on processes rather than outcomes, and on customer satisfaction. Thomas Stewart portrays the case of reengineering at GTE, which set up its first "customer care center" last year. The traditional job of GTE repair clerks was to record information from a customer, fill out a trouble ticket, and send it on to others who tested lines and switches until they found and fixed the problem. Instead GTE wanted to complete repairs while the customer was still on the phone, something that prior to the reengineering happened just once in two hundred calls. The first step was to move testing and switching equipment to the desks of the repair clerks, now called front-end technicians, who were given training in how to use their new tools. GTE stopped measuring how fast the technicians handled calls and instead tracked how often they cleared up a problem without passing it on. After the reengineering, problems are solved by a front-end technician three times out of ten, and GTE is shooting for upward of seven hits.[14]

The next step has been to link sales and billing with repairs, a task GTE is doing with push-button-phone menus that allow callers to connect directly to any service. Operators have been given new software to access data bases that allow them to handle virtually any customer request. As a result, GTE has witnessed a 20 percent to 30 percent increase in productivity. From a motivational perspective, reengineering at GTE has successfully resulted in a match between the company's objective to improve customer service and the employees' goal to satisfy their need for self-growth.

Parallel to U.S. creation of job design programs focusing on changing individual jobs, an approach known as *autonomous work groups* (or the sociotechnical system), has been developed at the team level in Britain, Sweden, and Norway. This approach is based on the assumption that work is commonly performed by teams, rather than by individuals who are independent of one another. The approach aims at integrating the social and technical aspects of the work system. The autonomous work groups almost always implement Hackman and Oldham's five principles of individual job design but at a group level—team autonomy, team responsibility, group feedback on performance, and task meaningfulness for the team. One of the criticisms of the sociotechnical system approach from an American viewpoint is that it does not adequately deal with differences between employees. However, this criticism conveys the individualistic value of American society, which is more concerned with recognizing individual talents than with group welfare.

In northern Europe, where the dominant cultural values are egalitarian and relatively more collectivistic than in west Europe, job enrichment has taken the form of autonomous work groups and sociotechnical systems. Perhaps the most famous of these projects were implemented in the Volvo auto plants in Kalmar and Uddevalla during the 1980s. Although these plants were shut down in 1993 and 1994 due to disastrous markets and low capacity utilization, they still serve as excellent examples of the benefits and limitations of the autonomous work groups.[15]

The major purposes of using autonomous work groups at Volvo was to attract a high-quality labor force while reducing absenteeism and turnover rates. Turnover at the Kalmar and Uddevalla plants had reached an excess of 20 percent, in contrast to a 12 percent rate in assembly plants of American car makers and only 5 percent in Japanese car factories.[16] By adopting a new form of work design, Volvo hoped to reduce these levels and increase efficiency by "humanizing" the nature of work and making it meaningful.

Work in the Kalmar plant was organized into major units, each performed by teams of employees. Each team was responsible for assembling a major portion of the car (e.g., electrical systems, interiors, and so forth) and for quality inspection. In addition, group members developed multiple skills that allowed them to rotate among themselves and substitute for each other. Responsibility for a major portion of the car enhanced task identity, and self-inspection created immediate feedback. Traditional assembly line practice has two significant detrimental effects. First quality is checked by specialists, often after the product is fully assembled. The employees are removed from the evaluation process and may never find out that their work was below expectation. Any feedback they receive is often nonspecific; they are told what defect rate for a day or week or month, but are not advised what to do differently in the future. Moreover, the greater the time interval between the work and the receipt of feedback, the less likely that there will be changes in behavior. Second, it may be significantly more expensive to rework or repair a quality problem after it has progressed further in the assembly process. In the Kalmar plant, the synchronization of the technical manufacturing process with team-focused production methods served to improve employee perceptions of their self-worth and well-being.

In the Uddevalla plant, each of eight parallel production teams took full responsibility for assembling the vehicle from subsystems up—a work cycle of about two hours. The teams largely managed themselves, handling scheduling, quality control, hiring, and other duties. There were only two organizational levels, shop-floor and plant management. In addition, there were significant improvements in working conditions to reduce the physical strain.

The results in both plants showed a significant improvement in employee morale, turnover was reduced to 6 percent, and quality was high. In addition, Uddevalla quality surpassed Volvo's main assembly plant in Gothenburg, Sweden, and the Volvo 940 model assembled at Uddevalla, Kalmar, and Gothenburg, was ranked the best European car. The short feedback loops enhanced team learning, and productivity progress at Uddevalla was remarkable. In 1992, the number of hours required per car decreased dramatically from fifty to thirty six hours, an amount of time similar to that in Kalmar and to that in average European car assembly plants. By these standards, one could say that the autonomous work groups in these plants were a success.

However, during the same period, the number of hours per car in U.S. assembly line plants was between twenty two and twenty five hours and in Japan was seventeen hours per car. These figures call into question the success just described. One explanation for the lower production rate was that although Uddevalla plant was designed for as many as forty eight assembly teams, it had only thirty five due to the dramatic decrease in sales. Further, each team could slow or accelerate the rate at which it received the parts. Since there was no pressure from the market to produce more cars, the teams may not have seen a reason to accelerate the pace of work to full capacity.

What can managers learn from the Volvo experience?

1. Autonomous work groups, compared with the assembly line, humanize the workplace. They attract high-quality employees and reduce the rate of turnover.

2. Autonomous work groups allow employees to assume responsibility, to learn and develop their skills, and to have a sense of task meaningfulness and self-worth. The design of teamwork fits best with the cultural characteristics of group focus and low power differential.

3. The quality level improves as a result of the high motivation and skill development.

4. The effect on the quantity level is not clear cut. On the one hand, the figures show that the number of hours per car was much lower in American and Japanese assembly line plants; yet the Volvo plants did not work at full capacity because of poor market conditions and a significant decrease in sales. Even then, the number of hours per car was similar to that of other European assembly-line car plants.

The development of individual job enrichment in the United States, autonomous work groups in North Europe, and quality control circles in Japan is not a coincidence. It demonstrates that different cultures create forms of motivational techniques congruent with dominant cultural values. Such motivational techniques are more likely to be accepted and to be regarded as providing opportunities for the experience of self-worth and well-being because they are consistent with cultural values.

The Horizontal Corporation

When employees' jobs have more autonomy, responsibility, and meaningfulness, we have a *horizontal corporation.* The horizontal corporation is an effective way to push authority down the organizational ladder and increase the level of shared responsibility through redesigning the company. "Forget the pyramid, smash hierarchy, break company into its key processes, and create teams from different departments to run them"—this is the essence of the new design of the horizontal corporation.[17] Horizontal organizations obviously work best in egalitarian cultures with low levels of power differential, such as the United States, Australia, Britain, the Netherlands, Sweden, and Norway. Similarly, horizontal organizations are less likely to emerge in cultures of high power differential like Japan, Korea, Singapore, Brazil, and India.

In egalitarian and self-focused cultures, authority is pushed down to the individual employees, whereas in egalitarian and group-focused cultures authority and responsibility are shared by the teams. Empowered employees satisfy self-enhancement and self-efficacy more than employees who do not have the authority to make decisions. In the traditional hierarchical organizational design, many layers of management slow down decision making and lead to high coordination costs: subordinates look up to bosses, and they do not have the autonomy to accommodate the immediate needs of their customers.

In an attempt to improve customer service, some of corporate America's biggest names, from American Telephone & Telegraph, to General Electric, to Motorola, are moving toward a horizontal design. The seven key elements of the horizontal corporation are

1. *Organize around process, not task.* Instead of relying on functional departments, a company should create three to five core processes with specific performance goals: (a) processes run by the top executive team, (b) processes of new-product development, (c) processes of production and sales, (d) processes of customer support.

2. *Flatten the hierarchy to reduce supervision.* Push responsibility and authority down the organizational ladder, and eliminate work activities that fail to add value.

3. *Make customer satisfaction the primary driver and measure of performance.*

4. *Maximize employees' contact with suppliers and customers.* Add suppliers and customer representatives as full working members of in-house teams when they can be of service.

5. *Inform and train all employees.*

6. *Make teams the main building block of the organization.* Limit direct supervision by making teams manage themselves. Give teams a common purpose, and hold them accountable for measurable performance goals.

7. *Reward team performance, not just individual performance.* Encourage employees to develop multiple skills rather than specialized know-how, and reward them for it.

The last two points of team orientation are going to be more effective in group-focused cultures than in self-focused ones.

Eastman Chemical converted its pyramidal organizational chart into a pizza chart to show that everyone is equal in that organization. PepsiCo flipped its pyramidal organizational chart upside down; to help focus on customers, Pepsi put its field representatives at the top. The horizontal organization meets the competitive demands of the twenty-first century, and more and more companies seem to be moving in this direction. This form of organization is going to emerge in cultures of low power differential. In the self-focused cultures, the horizontal organization is going to enhance personal responsibility and accountability. In group-focused cultures, responsibility and accountability are going to reside in the team.

Summary

The work of managers is manifested through the work of others. Managers rely on their subordinates for the attainment of their organizational goals. Therefore managers must develop an awareness of the underlying motives of their employees, an understanding of their values, and knowledge of the motivational techniques that provide opportunities for experiencing self-worth and well-being. In particular, global managers need to be aware of the way cultural values affect how workers evaluate the meaning of various motivational techniques. These values are shaped to a great extent by cultural characteristics and differ greatly. Varying criteria are used in different cultures for evaluating the opportunities provided by various motivational techniques for self-fulfillment. A group versus a self-focus and a high versus low power differential form value systems that affect the way rewards are allocated, decisions are made, and jobs and organizations are designed.

6

Making a Group into a Team

This chapter focuses on effective teams—their formation and maintenance. We provide a brief background on the team as it exists in an organization as well as a general way of looking at team processes across cultures. Finally, we present a number of applications of our model to topics in team dynamics such as conformity and stimulating creativity, team decisions, motivation of team members, and combination of the team with technological innovations.

Why do we form into teams, and what is their function in an effective company? In many U.S. corporations, teams are formed at the initiative of management to solve management, production, sales, and other problems as to help the company maintain a competitive edge. For instance, Ed Lawler of the University of Southern California surveyed Fortune 1,000 companies and found that the amount of management-initiated teamwork has increased substantially from 1987 to the present.[1] He argues that companies using a "high involvement," or team-based approach are among the most effective. People also voluntarily join teams in order to satisfy their self-motives and cultural values, and they do so with people similar to themselves. In some countries like Germany and Sweden, work teams are organized through national labor laws in a system of participative management. Regardless of why people join a team, a key question is how do we transform a group of employees into a successful team? What will be clear from this chapter is that creating an effective team is tied to our self-knowledge and our cultural background. The tasks chosen by teams, their approach to work, and the rewards associated with their functioning vary according to cultural values. It is essential to the understand that not only do different motives, aligned with cultural background, operate in teams but also the same motives may be satisfied very differently according to team members' cultures. Regardless of the work to be done, the culture, or the members' motives, the key to a successful team hinges on the team leader's awareness of how to synergistically combine these elements.

A Tale of Two Very Different Teams

In 1979, Bill Walsh was named head coach of the San Francisco 49ers, a football team that had little promise and had been picked apart and mismanaged during the 1970s. The team lacked direction and was devoid of consistent talent. What did Walsh do? He immediately began to implement a unique vision and long-range strategic plan for his new team using a variety of new methods for training and preparing his team. These techniques included a micromanagement approach rarely seen in the National Football League (NFL), such as choreographing and detailing his players' practices, defining specific play contingency plans for the game, and setting detailed objectives for all of the players, assistant coaches, and coaches. What was the result? Walsh has taken his team to three superbowl championships and has turned a losing team into one of the greatest teams in NFL history, one so strong that some sports commentators have stated that it would never have a loosing season under Walsh.[2] Walsh has used a variety of techniques and approaches to his team building that are noteworthy because they are uniquely adapted to the individualistic spirit of American football. Walsh believes, for instance, in rigorously planning out the individual actions of each team member during a game in order that everyone is prepared for any possible turn of events. Although this approach places a rather heavy individual burden on this players, Walsh says that it is worth the effort. In this regard he comments:

> Making judgments under severe stress is the most difficult thing there is. The more preparation you have prior to the conflict, the more you can do in a clinical situation, the better off you will be. For that reason, in practice I want to make certain that we have accounted for every critical situation, including the desperate ones at the end of a game when we may have only one chance to pull out a victory. Even in that circumstance, I want us to have a play prepared and rehearsed. Say it

is the last twenty seconds of a game, and we're losing. We have already practiced six plays that we can apply in that situation. That way, we know what to do, and we can calmly execute the plays. We'll have no doubt in our minds, we will have more poise, and we can concentrate without falling prey to desperation.

What this approach means from his players' viewpoint is a tremendous amount of hard work and practice as well as a great deal of remembering plays, plans, and actions. More important, it demonstrates Walsh's heavy emphasis on a team built on the shoulders of individuals and individual responsibility.

Walch cites as an example his work with superstar quarterback Joe Montana. Walsh recalls:

Early on, we had to encourage Joe to trust his spontaneous instincts. We were careful not to criticize him when he used his creative abilities and things did not work out. In practice, we worked with Joe repeatedly on specific plays. When he was placed in a game, we called only those plays because we knew that he should be confident that he could execute them. But we didn't jump him the minute he would break the pattern. Instead, we nurtured him to use his instincts. We had to allow him to be wrong on occasion and to live with it.

Coach Walsh has built his team using other means as well. For instance, he focuses his efforts on developing the "middle six" players out of any ten. The middle six refers to those who are not yet playing to their full potential, who have the talent to get better. Rather than focusing on remedial training for the bottom few or wasting effort pushing superstars already at their peak, Walsh organizes the team and emphasizes improving those who will most benefit from his coaching.

An important lesson, for a self-focused culture like America, that Walsh shows us is that a team effort does not mean that the individual disappears from view. There is always an important balance between the individual and his or her group or team.

Another important lesson that we get from Walsh's team development concerns the exit of team members. Walsh is careful not to let tenure become permanent if it threatens the team's welfare; he will make the painful decision of letting past superstars go when the time comes. Walsh emphasizes, however, that the exit must be accomplished in such a way that the veteran retains his dignity and self-esteem and must also minimize the impact of the transition on the rest of the team. This is an interesting point as well: Walsh seeks to maintain the individual self-enhancement of players, even when they are no longer productive. Such an approach to "weeding the garden" is important for both those players leaving the team and those remaining, who may otherwise develop negative feelings. In other words, the "survivors" of cuts often experience a sense of loss (and a threat to self consistency) that can be reduced if each player leaving the team is treated as an important and unique contributor.

Now we turn our discussion to a very different type of team— namely, the Japanese women's Olympic volleyball team. This team, characterized as one of the most talented ever to play the sport, is often a dominating influence in the international arena. Led by a variety of coaches, the women's team is not labeled as anyone's particular creation; rather it is a group consisting of nearly interchangeable players. The structure and training that go into the nurturing of this highly successful team are far from individualized. Players are exposed to grueling training sessions during which they must field volleyballs hit at them time and time again. More important each player is expected to be strong in any position; no one is treated like a "star." Quite the contrary, players comment that anyone who wants to be treated differently is hurting the cohesiveness of the team. While Bill Walsh encourages individual initiative in his players, the Japanese volleyball coach breaks down personal variation in order that the team operates as a single unit. So extreme is this emphasis that one past coach would refer to the players by their position not by their name, during practice. Despite these dramatic management differences and philosophies of teams, the 49ers and the Japanese women's volleyball team have long, successful histories. We now unlock some of the secrets to these successes in relation to corporations.

As we have pointed out, employees do not work within a social void; instead, they interact and are dependent on others in their companies. People work together not just to perform their job but for social needs as well. In this chapter, we will look at how self-knowledge helps us understand the dynamics of a team with special attention to applications in work settings—improving team decisions, motivating people through team recognition, and stimulating individual initiative in a team setting.

What Are Teams?

How prevalent are teams? All we have to do is to look around us to see how essential team activities are to us. Our lives are organized around many teams (families, work committees, religions, sports, etc.). Much of what we do for business and pleasure revolves around the team. This is not to say that whatever we do occurs within a team; sometimes we work by ourselves, and sometimes we work in *groups* but not *teams*. Whereas a team has a sense of community and loyalty (and specific roles and structure), simple groups refer to a collection of individuals who gather for personal reasons and needs (for example an audience at a movie).

Joseph McGrath of the University of Illinois emphasizes that teams differ from other social aggregates in as much as the latter do not have the potential mutual interaction of a group.[3] In other words, a team has several identifying characteristics. First, it is usually small so that all members can talk and interact with one another. Second, team members are dependent on one another, and they must take into consideration other members' choices and decisions as they themselves act. Third, this mutual dependence implies that the team has a history and continues over time with an expected future. This definition of a team includes families (at least the residential unit core), work crews, and many social or friendship groups but does not include groups that fit other kinds of collections of people—communities or entire companies. Thus we can distinguish a team from other groups of people based on three dimensions: size, mutual dependence, and longevity.

We have already seen that people rely on their teams to various degrees based on their self-knowledge and cultural values. Robert Bontempo of Columbia University and his colleagues, for example, looked at the importance of team identification and goals for Brazilians and Americans. Both publicly and confidentially they asked people how likely and how desirable it would be for them to do some awkward or costly act for a team member (e.g., visit a sick friend in the hospital). Americans publicly said that they would take on the burden but confidentially stated that they were unlikely to do so; even if they did go, they would not enjoy doing so. The Brazilians (team-focused) did not differ in their public and confidential responses; they reported that they would go to the hospital and that they would likely enjoy doing so. This finding suggests that team membership and the norms that emerge for members vary across cultures, and so do the features that guide our choice of teams.

Team Processes

In keeping with our self-knowledge approach, we have outlined a more specific way of thinking about teams in Figure 6.1. We begin by looking at how loose collections of people turn into teams. If you

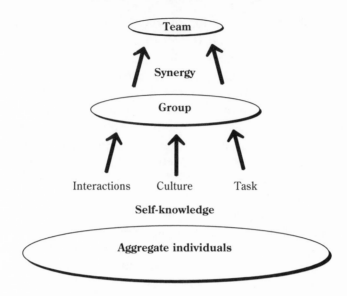

Figure 6.1 *A model of aggregates, groups and teams*

understand this process, then you can take the correct steps to make certain that you always have a successful team. Notice that self-knowledge and culture are at the base of the figure (along with interactions and task). Thus to build an effective team, you must coordinate self-knowledge, culture, ways of interacting, and the work to be done.

The figure is a guide for describing the differences among teams and the ways teams form and operate. There are important differences between loose aggregates of people, groups, and teams. We place the team at the top of our figure because it refers to a very special collection of people. A team reflects a synergy in which the sum of the individual pieces (team members) is overshadowed by the unique combination of the team members' talents and inputs. In this section, we describe the *process* of how a loose collection of people becomes a team using three phases.

Phase 1: Is This the Right Team For Me?

The team-building process begins with how people view them-selves and how this view influences their decisions to join par-ticular teams. Why does an employee choose a specific team? Of course, employees are often assigned to their work groups by management in order to get some specific work completed. At Rockwell International, teamwork is strongly emphasized with teams being defined by functional departments within a given business. However, Rockwell gives these departments the freedom to include key personnel from other departments if needed. These cross-functional teams can even involve employees from different business units (such as a member from the aerospace division working with a team from the heavy-manufacturing unit [Allen Bradley]. In a number of group-focused countries like Singapore, South Korea, and Japan, teams are formed by the employees as a normal part of management structure. For instance, Daihatsu's automobile manufacturing uses shop-floor work teams that are formed by employees working on common activities (e.g., engine assembly). These teams are so ingrained into the culture that they permeate all parts of the company for nearly all work activities. In self-focused countries like Canada or Britain, people do not always seek out teams unless encouraged by their organization. However, if given freedom to choose and a bit of encouragement from management, people will join teams that satisfy their three self-motives. In other words, an employee who has a strong motive for self-enhancement will likely seek out a team that has prestige and success, or an employee who is very high on self-consistency will look for stable and mature teams that do not experience a great deal of turbulence and change. If an employee cannot find a good match, then she or he will continue searching using self-knowledge as a guide for finding the right team.

What about team membership and a person's cultural values? People from a self-focused culture like the United States will join a number of teams and move among them freely in order to satisfy their self-motives. As the demands of a particular team become cumbersome, the self-focused employee will shift attention to other, less demanding, team memberships. At the same time, the self-focused team member will be receptive to others because he or she doesn't know whether the stranger may end up being a future group member! This fact is why Americans are often referred to as universal partners in business. By contrast, in a group-focused culture such as Japan, people's teams are stable over time, an individual's membership is often dictated by schooling and other background characteristics, and people have relatively few memberships. The result is that forming new teams in a group-focused culture can be difficult; a manager is faced with putting people into teams who are not used to multiple memberships.

Phase 2: How Should I Act?

Once a match is made, we enter the next phase of the team building process. In this second phase, a collection of individuals begin to work together as a group as a result of socializing new members. People get to know one another, and they develop a sense of roles, and status in the team.

Phase 3: What Will the Team Get Me
and What Can I Do for It?

The final part of our model refers to the outcomes that the team achieves and to team interaction. These outcomes include productivity as well as how well team members get along both with one another and with other teams. For example, a highly task-oriented team may insulate itself from others with the intention of being productive. This isolation, however, might be viewed as competitive or even malevolent by interrelated teams who might in turn isolate the team from needed resources. Eventually the once-productive team may become unproductive because it lacks resources from others. Recall our discussion of General Motor's Saturn division and the negative reactions to its success from other GM units (e.g., Chevrolet) and from senior GM management.

The relationship between teams from self- and group-focused cultures is not the same. In a self-focused culture, even competing teams will often respect one another's boundaries, and they rarely compete to the point of hurting themselves. A very different picture develops in a group-focused culture—membership is long term and stable, and there is more concern with the internal workings of a team than with how other teams function. In fact, teams from a group-focused culture may compete with one another to an extreme, even if it potentially harms themselves. Without question, teams from a group-focused culture will compete with one another (and with teams from other cultures) in a seemingly tough and calculating fashion by typical American standards.

A team's outcomes will have an influence on a member's desire to seek out new team memberships as well, especially in a self-focused culture. If a person's self-motives are left unfulfilled, he or she will search for new affiliations in many cases.[4] Of course, the opportunity and the determination to change teams varies according to company and culture. For example, a person from a self-focused country whose self-motives are unsatisfied may change teams (or expand into new ones while keeping old memberships active), but a person from a team-focused country will not likely do so. Instead the latter will try and change the existing team. Why is this? As we have mentioned, people from group-focused countries often are born into their teams, and there is a strong emphasis placed on team membership and stability. A traveler to mainland China commented on an incident that he had experienced on a train. It seems that a young woman manager (Chinese) from Shenzen boarded the first-class car, having paid for a sleeper compartment. She was refused admittance even though she had paid for the room in advance. Why? The train conductor said that she was not of the right "importance,"—that is to say, high enough in the government or a foreign tourist. What was even more interesting was that the woman eventually agreed with the conductor that she had been mistaken in taking the liberty of breaking rank.

Now that we have covered the basics concerning team processes, we will turn our attention to using this knowledge to transform collections of individuals into effective teams.

Moving from an Aggregate to a Group to a Team

Forming a Strong Team

Assuming that we do indeed want to move to a team approach to work, how can we do so? What are the secrets that Bill Walsh used with the 49ers or Bill Gates at Microsoft? We will now turn to a general set of guidelines that can help a manager transform an aggregate of employees into a team. As we proceed, we will describe how these steps must be adapted to satisfy various cultural and self-knowledge demands.

STEP 1: OUT OF MANY, ONE
People must understand that as members of a team they depend on one another for success.

Our first step is for people to have a strong sense that they are one team and not many individuals. Is identification with a team really important to its cohesiveness? Yes, a team must be able to identify itself as unique, and its members must share a common identity. How is this achieved? Although identifying with the team is always very important, a manager uses different approaches to accomplish this goal in various cultures. In many self-focused countries, such simple things as coffee cups and T-shirts with company logos can help establish a team's sense of unique identity. An engineer from Intel told the American author that one of the "fun" parts of going to a big trade show is that he can collect free gifts (like T-shirts, book bags, etc.) given out at the various companies' booths. He also said that the sign of a successful company is that they give away interesting and good-quality gifts. These curios help a self-focused team member show others her or his team, they emphasize that it is almost a possession of the person.

There are a number of things that we can do to achieve this feeling. (1) We can get people together in a common area and separate from other teams. (2) We can develop a common team "theme" and logo to represent its particular identity. (3) We can bring together people who are alike. (4) We can demonstrate to team members their mutual interdependence through small team activities. One of the finest examples of this approach is exemplified by the Apple Macintosh planning/product team. In order to develop an entirely new product, former CEO Steve Jobs took a hand-picked design team away from the main Apple building (literally left the main building to isolate the team) and put it in a special "creativity" zone so that it could work uninterrupted by the mainstream of the company. Other companies will take somewhat less drastic approaches that allow teams or product divisions to go away for a weekend in order to build a stronger sense of "teamness." This first guideline is clearly more important in a self- than in a group-focused culture; people from a self-focused culture, like the United States, are not used to submerging their individual personalities to that of their group. A manager must reassure self-focused employees that they are important and unique contributors to the team. Again, if we think about the Macintosh example, we see that the design-team approach taken at Apple emphasized the uniqueness of both the team and its members. The team never became more important than its members.

Step 2: Developing a Cohesive Team

Team members must have a strong desire to stay with the team and commit themselves to it.

The second step is to make the team cohesive. A highly cohesive team has members who are willing to "go the extra mile" for one another. How can we improve team cohesiveness? There are a number of ways to do so.

1. We can help team members understand the important and singular contributions that they can make to satisfy their self-enhancement and self-efficacy motives.

2. We can increase the needs that team membership can satisfy.

3. We can monitor and evaluate the degree to which members satisfy these needs to make certain their motives are turned into action.

4. We can give team members a chance to make sacrifices for the team. Logically cohesiveness increases when we feel we are making an important, individual contribution to team success.

The last point, making sacrifices, reflects a basic fact of psychology: if we suffer or sacrifice for something, we will value it more in the future. Why is this statement true? If we are willing to give or ourselves in order to achieve some target, then we *must have* wanted the target outcome. Sacrifice for the team creates commitment.[5] Is it any wonder that college fraternities and sororities use hazing and that the military has its bootcamp?

Creating a coherent team in a group-focused culture is easy if the members have common characteristics and backgrounds. In Japanese companies, there is a strong unity within any single organization, and cohesive teams can be formed easily. A special challenge for a Japanese manager occurs when he or she tries to form teams with both Japanese and non-Japanese employees since this practice violates cultural rules of a closed society. One way to overcome this dilemma is for the Japanese manager to emphasize that all of the members are part of the same company, that the company is the common bond.

Step 3: Creating an Active Concern About the Team

It is important that all members are concerned about the team and its fate.

The third step is to engender a sense of mutual fate concern about the team. How do we do this? (1) We develop guidelines and standards for the team to use. (2) We encourage the team to follow these guidelines by rewarding such action through praise and recognition. (3) We help team members to take pride in their actions to satisfy their self-enhancement motive. For instance, at Hong Kong Metro Transportation Railways, employees are encouraged to work with one another and report potential problems as well as existing ones. What has emerged from this system is that shift members who work together will take pride of accomplishment even if their fellow shift worker(s) help improve the provision of transportation service. In other words the team-focused Chinese workers are using one another's accomplishments as a source of pride. In contrast, the best way to develop this concern in a self-focused culture like the United States and Canada is to tie each member's personal success to that of the team's. An American will be concerned about the team as long as it is satisfying the member's self-motives.

Making the Team More Effective

Once a manager has established the basic team, the job has really just begun. Teams are like flowers beginning to bud—they must be watered and nurtured for them to blossom. What's more, they need to be cared for if they are to see another season. Here are the steps needed to make a team more effective.

First, a manager must work with a team in order to establish *useful standards* for the team. These standards can be enforced in a number of ways: (1) generating the standards through team inter-action; (2) aligning team standards with the unique self-motives of team members; (3) getting individual sacrifice for the team's needs; (4) making sanctions for violating team standards clear and strong; and (5) developing a monitoring system through which individual team members' contributions to the whole can be assessed.[6]

To see a team's standards as transient and malleable, however, provides an incomplete picture: it ignores the individual's own personal standards for action based on his or her own culture. An example will demonstrate our point. A German manager was sent to run a large, luxury hotel in Guangzhou, China. One of his first observations was that the desk clerks seemed to spend a great deal of time talking with one another and quite a bit less time helping hotel guests who approached the front desk. He interpreted this as rudeness on the part of the Chinese clerks, and he fired a number of people and reprimanded others. After these actions and a great deal of employee outcry, he was told by a Chinese manager that the clerks behavior reflected the view that interrupting a conversation with a friend in order to "serve" a customer (or stranger) is rude. Differences in cultural practices in this case led the German manager to misinterpret his Chinese employees.

Second, an effective team leader must *lead productive discussions* within the team. Sometimes the way we discuss matters is dictated by our culture. In the famous *ringi* system of decision making in Japan, team members gain consensual support for a decision by informally testing it out at increasing levels of their team so that everyone affected is committed to the decision. This process is culturally determined, and the lowest member in the chain has the role/obligation to move the decision up through the system. Yet we already know that this approach to communication and discussion is not universally applicable to teams with other standards and values. In the power and status hierarchy of South Korea, this form of decision making would not be appropriate since a subordinate would never assume a superior's authority and introduce a decision on his or her own. In this case, members within a team would work together in order to implement work goals given from the team's leader. The participation and cooperation come in when the Korean teams work together on an existing project or task, rather than the initiation of such a project.

As we discussed in Chapter 4, there are a number of important things that affect and facilitate communication within a team. First, a manager should encourage team members to take an active interest in contributing to team discussion. The manager can choose interesting discussion points (e.g., salient to team members) and pose an initial question in such a way that a simple yes or no answer is insufficient. For example, Bill Lindsey at Hughes Aircraft does not ask his work team, "Should we do 'X' next?" Rather he says "Now that we have finished the 'X' project, what should we do next?". The open-ended question with the initial reference to past projects encourages people to think about what would logically follow and cannot be answered by a simple response.

Another important way for a leader to manage team communication is to allow members time to respond. Often members may have ideas that are somewhat underdeveloped, and these evolve as discussion unfolds. A wise team leader will give key questions to members prior to the discussion so that they can think about the issues, and the leader lets people have some silent moments during discussion so that their ideas can gestate a bit. Even though silent periods may seem awkward and uncomfortable, they can be invaluable for team members. We might also remember that these quiet periods (and other patterns of discourse in a team's discussion) will reflect self-knowledge and culture. For instance, we have seen that it is considered quite inappropriate for a Korean worker to question a superior's statement or judgment. It is even difficult to solicit input from an employee because that person does not want contradict what a superior might say. In Italy, employees feel quite free to openly disagree with their superiors, and they will likely do so. Clearly the rules for soliciting discussion must be adapted to cultural practices. In countries with a high power distance, discussion must be carefully led by a team leader with an emphasis placed on letting people express themselves. Team members might be encouraged to meet with one another without the leader present to reduce the concern that their opinions might differ from those of the leader.

Still another consideration is that in each team there may be differences among members concerning their individual status, and these will have an impact on who discusses what and how discussion will proceed. We often think that status differences play little role in low power differential countries. For instance, in mainland China, there is an emphasis on general equality. In the United States, uniforms, badges, insignias, and the like clearly distinguish among ranks; in mainland China, military uniforms are the same, and differential insignias are not worn. This situation suggests a society with a very low power differential. However, according to the authors' conversations with former Chinese soldiers, the lack of insignias does not mean that differences in uniforms go completely unnoticed. The high-ranking officers often have uniforms made out of very fine cloth compared with infantry soldiers. These more subtle cues help guide the nature of interaction in a team such as who speaks to whom and when. A related example concerns the low-context culture of Japan, in which the very nature of the language conveys role and status as people speak with one another. Moreover, in Japanese culture, much of what happens is not actually said, but is conveyed by who speaks and by how something is said.

The third step for an effective team is to *develop goals* for its own action.[7] Of course, an effective team does not establish for itself unrealistically difficult goals since the likely outcome of these is failure and disillusionment. How can a team set useful goals for itself or how can a manager develop effective goals for subordinates? First, the team must monitor its own performance and productivity, so that it has a sense of what it can or cannot achieve. Second, team members must commit themselves to the goals through some means (e.g., team participation), and the importance of achieving these objectives must be emphasized. Third, interteam competition can be used to enhance a healthy spirit of competitiveness for more self-focused cultures. Finally, the team needs to focus on its work practices so as continually to improve on existing practices. (We discuss the importance of this continuous improvement focus in our chapter on quality and service.)

So far, we have emphasized the way that a team deals with its internal functioning. For the fourth step, we turn briefly to the way that an effective team deals with the *world around it*. How can a team cope with external pressures that it may face? To begin, we need to remember that each team faces outsiders who are themselves members of teams. These outsiders represent their own teams' and their personal interests as they place demands on other teams. Thus an important beginning is to understand the underlying goals and motives of outsiders and their respective teams. Here we draw on our self-knowledge and culture model. If we look at the actions and opinions expressed by these external agents, we can learn more about their motives. Why is Chevrolet, for instance, so aggressive in its attitude about its companion division Saturn? Perhaps it is threatened by its own lowered sales and is experiencing low enhancement. Another possibility is that the Saturn division represents a radical break from existing procedures, that threatens an entrenched way of thinking (in other words it threatens the consistency motive). A manager must consider the cultural ramifications of other teams' actions. People in a strong team-focused culture will view their own team membership as a long-term proposition; such individuals have intense and prolonged loyalty to their teams. As a result, we just may find that changing around team composition threatens more than just general familiarity with fellow team members.

So what can an effective team do to deal with the external environment? It can for example, avoid internal influence if possible, determine the other's source of power and see if it can be eroded, co-opt others to support the team's goals, ingratiate team members with others, who hold power, and become such an integral part of operations that other teams depend on it for their own effectiveness. This last point is particularly useful since it helps transform a "we versus they" attitude into one of mutual dependence and cooperation.

The fifth step concerns the way that *work and effort are rewarded* in an organization.[8] In an effective team, there are a number of ways that rewards can be distributed among members— equity, individual effort, equality, and need. What is relevant to our discussion is that the exchanges that occur within a team may be guided by several different rules and that these vary according to cultural values. For example, Kwok Leung and Michael Bond of the Chinese University of Hong Kong showed that in group-focused cultures, such as China and Taiwan, equity or equality distribution rules are preferred, depending on whether a person is dealing with the person's own team or another team. When dealing with their own teams, Chinese managers prefer to use an equality norm for giving out rewards, whereas in dealing with people from another team they followed a strong equity norm.

Of course, the rewards that are given out in a team must be tailored to the needs of the individual members as well. Recall that Bill Walsh said that he nurtured Joe Montana according to the quarterback's specific traits. Walsh made certain that he reinforced the reliance of Montana on his own instincts, something that he seemed hesitant to do himself. The important point is that the effectiveness of a team depends on whether its members are rewarded according to their personal and cultural need preferences. Remember, we are not talking about "need" per se, but about rewards that are actually desired by the members.

There is a more subtle aspect of reward and effort in an effective team that has been discussed by Allan Lind and Tom Tyler.[9] These researchers have demonstrated that the way rewards are allocated is important. In this case we are referring to the *procedures* used—and the people who have a say in deciding those procedures. Lind and Tyler have found that if given an opportunity to voice their opinions about reward distribution (even if these are not accepted), team members will feel better about the rewards that they do get. Having a say reinforces the idea that a person is a valued member of the team.

We would also expect cultural variations in what people expect in terms of having a say in their team's functioning as well as satisfaction with it. In a highly group-focused culture, of course, team members already give their input. Try *not* giving a Swede or an Israeli the opportunity to express an opinion and see what happens! However, this kind of participation may have a stronger impact in a more self-focused culture, where such opportunities emphasize the importance of each member as a unique person.

Continuing to Improve Team Effectiveness

In this section, we describe a number of different team dynamics and suggest how they relate to our effective team management. Our listing of topics is not exhaustive, but our intention is to present a number of examples so that a manager can guide a team to success in any cultural situation.

Conformity and Stimulating Creativity in a Team

Why are people socialized? The purpose of socialization is to assure that people will conform to a society's, an organization's, or a team's practices. Conformity is an important element in work and teams, but obviously it can stifle individual initiative and creativity. A challenge for a manager is to balance the need for people in a team to work in unison, while retaining their unique contributions.

Research on conformity has often looked at the impact of people's mere presence on the type of judgments that a person may make. For instance, Whittaker and Meade have examined the extent to which people from Brazil, Hong Kong, Lebanon, and Rhodesia conform to peer pressure.[10] In each of the four countries, people were placed in a group in which all the other members answered a question a certain (and incorrect) way. What the people put in these groups didn't realize is that the other members were in cahoots with the researchers and purposefully gave the same wrong answers. The researchers found that people in this study conformed to the group standard at about the same rate as Americans, with roughly one-third of the people giving the group-endorsed answer. In the case of the Bantu tribes people of Rhodesia, over one-half of the people conformed. Other research conducted in Germany and Japan showed similar results, although surprisingly there appears to be lower conformity in Japan than in the United States. A famous Japanese saying, "The nail that sticks out is hammered down," suggests that conformity should be *higher* in Japan than in the United States. One reason for this unexpected result may be that the temporary teams used in these studies didn't capture real, ongoing teams that are so important for the Japanese (and other team-focused cultures) and team members consisted of groups of strangers, not friends.

Using our self-knowledge approach, we can understand why people conform by looking at their self-consistency motive and team loyalty. Put simply, people conform because they want to maintain consistency in their actions with others and because they desire to remain a respected team member. The actual amount of conformity that exists will depend on both of these factors. In a group-focused culture, some people who have a low need for consistency may still conform since their desire to maintain team membership is high. In a self-focused culture, some people with a high need for consistency may nevertheless decide to leave the team. Conformity will likely change as a function of the work that people perform; jobs that promote high mutual dependence (like a computer design team) will likely increase conformity as a way to coordinate members' actions.

How can a manager overcome the inertia of conformity in order to stimulate creativity within a team? Again, the methods available to a manager depend on the self-motives of the team-members and on their cultural orientation. Coach Walsh saw that Montana had a strong self-efficacy (growth) motive but that he was timid about taking initiative. Consistent with a self-focused culture, Walsh focused on rewarding Montana's initiatives even if they were not successful. He provided Montana with the specific plays and guidelines but encouraged and recognized his individual actions. What about a strong power- and status-oriented culture like India or Singapore? Team creativity can best be stimulated through a strong paternalistic role by the recognized team leader.

Improving Team Decisions

As previously noted one of the most important management techniques is to discuss participation in the decision-making process as a means of enhancing team members' acceptance of and commitment to a decision. This team-decision method is highly effective in changing people's attitudes and work habits. A second aspect of decision making is the so-called risky shift, a problem in making good decisions. A number of years ago, an executive attending the Sloan business school and several of his professors discovered that teams made more extreme judgments (toward risk or caution depending on the decision to be made) than individuals. He showed his fellow executives some business problems that needed to be solved, such as making an investment in a politically unstable country. He found that they tended to make very risky decisions as a team. This outcome was particularly surprising since many people thought that teams had a conservative, or conforming, influence on decisions.

Why do these shifts occur? Individuals shift toward the extremes of risk and caution (according to their cultural values) in order to look capable. One researcher has examined this question with a team of Liberians, who culturally value caution over risk. The Liberians made more cautious than risky decisions consistent with their cultural values and with both the self-consistency and self-enhancement motives. In a high risk-taking culture, the motives of self-efficacy and enhancement would result in more shifts toward risk than caution. In this culture, risk-oriented decisions help fulfill the growth opportunities sought by team members.

How can a team improve its decision making and avoid these risky and cautious extremes?

1. Members of the team can present their ideas and opinions concerning a decision independently or even in written form.

2. The self-motives of each team member should be considered. Members having a strong self-efficacy motive, for instance, should focus on generating plans for action while being cautioned about being overly committed to taking on great challenges.

3. Teams need to avoid premature consensus in their decisions, particularly in a group-focused culture. One way of doing so is through the use of a devil's advocate, or dissenting member, who takes the role of disagreeing with or questioning the general flow of the team's discussion.

Motivating Team Member Performance

We can also look at the nature of team from the perspective of low and high performers. In the case of the high contributors, we make note of *social facilitation,* or the tendency for people to perform better when they are in front of others than when they are by themselves. Do we usually perform better with people watching us? The answer is both yes and no. Having others watch us as we work energizes us, and it activates our self-motives by making us more self-aware. The result is an increase in energy that translates into better performance for jobs that people already do well. However, being watched has a harmful effect on unfamiliar jobs. From a cultural viewpoint, a facilitation effect depends on several factors, such as the relative importance of self-enhancement, team membership, and performance norms. A person coming from a culture familiar with teamwork, like a Volvo auto worker, will not experience the same level of increased motivation because he or she is used to working in a team.

A related but opposite effect of a team on individual efforts is called *social loafing.* Social loafing means that people don't work as hard as part of a team as by themselves. Mancur Olson of the University of Maryland argued that as a team's size increases, an individual's feelings of dispensability also increases and personal effort diminishes. Because her or his effort may go unnoticed, the person will redirect effort from the team's task to pursue personal goals. As a result, the person gets both the team's rewards as well as other personal rewards. Since any specific contribution to a team is increasingly difficult to monitor as team size increases, the person is less likely to get caught loafing. Of course, this argument is based on a self-focused culture (the United States) in which people put their individual gain ahead of that of the team.

A few studies of social loafing have been conducted in cultures other than the United States. For instance, some researchers found a facilitation effect of team-based performance for Taiwanese and Hong Kong students. They found that a team setting actually *increased* members' performances. Tamao Matsui and his colleagues in Japan looked at the differential effect of individual and team responsibility for work performance. They found that a team-based approach was superior to an individually based one in their study.[11]

The first author of our book has looked at social loafing in group-focused and self-focused managers coming from mainland China, Hong Kong, Israel, and the United States. He has discovered that loafing occurs for people in a self-focused culture (e.g., the Americans) but not for people in a group-focused culture (e.g., the Chinese and Israelis). In follow-up work, he has found that loafing does not occur for people in a group-focused culture if they work with their team but does happen if they work alone or in an group of strangers. People from a self-focused culture loaf regardless of team membership but do not loaf when they work by themselves.

Self-knowledge suggests several reasons for these findings. Most obviously team membership seems to be more effective in making people from a group-focused culture think about concepts of survival and efficacy than people in a self-focused culture. Perhaps the most important finding is simply that culture and self-knowledge both play an important role in determining whether or not people will loaf.

Assume for a minute that you are a manager in a country prone to social loafing such as the United States or Britain. What can you do? To begin, recognize that loafing occurs because a person's individual efforts go unnoticed in the team; this is why individual accountability is so important . Each person must realize that his or her contribution is unique and essential. Accountability is *not* just for sake of monitoring or policing people's efforts; accountability means that people *know that they count*. As Olson reveals, another reason for loafing is that people seek personal rewards on team time, probably because the team is not satisfying the person's needs. It is therefore important that the team offer the member adequate self-fulfillment. Finally, loafing may occur if a team member thinks that he or she is being played for a "sucker." In other words, people may loaf if they believe that others are doing the same. Of course, the answer here is to make certain that everyone puts in a fair share of effort, perhaps by making public at staff meetings each person's work contributions.

Work Teams

A final topic that we will address concerns work teams as they relate to technological innovations. This topic is sufficiently voluminous that we provide a detailed discussion in other chapters; we will focus here on a few issues in order to illustrate some general principles.

First, a great deal of attention has been focused on the use of individually versus team-based designs of jobs. Should we design jobs so that they complement the needs of a single employee, or should we design them from the perspective of the team? The focus of much of this work has been on the approach to job design used in the Scandanavian countries. This concentrates on maintaining intact teams by integrating the technology with team needs. The idea is to allow team members more discretion in their work, provide them control over their nonwork activities, and so forth. The advantage of this approach for group-focused cultures is that natural teams are maintained so workers do not become alienated.

In a self-focused culture, however, we know that self-efficacy and individual growth are achieved through individual accomplishment rather than team effort. Consistent with this idea, there is the job design model, which we mentioned in Chapter 2. This approach looks at the redesign of work from an individual's perspective. As with its group-focused counterpart, emphasis is placed on merging of technology/work with human needs, but it emphasizes individual requirements, such as personal autonomy and knowledge of results. Again, we can see that such an approach will be effective to the extent that it satisfies the desire for personal growth.

A second area is the work conducted on management systems referred to as quality circles, which we have mentioned earlier and will return to later. Quality circles stress quality control techniques that are taught to all employees and that provide opportunities for participation. Although some critics suggest that this participation can be coercive, the system does provide prestige, occupational opportunities, and limited financial incentives through bonuses.

The basic principle of the quality circle is the provision of team-based suggestions for the improvement of the work environment and production. What is unique is that the system appears to enhance worker commitment and loyalty. And since quality control is taught to all employees, manufacturing rejection rates are low and fewer product inspectors required.

From our team and self-knowledge models, we can see a number of facets that apply to the quality circle principle and suggest that it may be useful in a number of different cultures (but for different reasons). The success of the quality circle technique is consistent with the ideological orientation of group-focused cultures

Table 6.1

Summary of Effective Team Structure and
Characteristics in Various Cultures

	Low Power Differential	High Power Differential
Self-focused	Loosely connected with ample opportunity for individual initiative and recognition. Teams should be self-governed, have open communi cation, and not place excessive demands on any team member.	Loosely connected with ample opportunity for individual recognition but not initiative. Guidance is given from superiors and communication is often downward. The teams should not place many demands on any team member.
	Examples: United States, New Zealand, Finland	Examples: South Africa, Italy, Spain
Group-focused	Tightly connected people with an equal say in all work activities, team goals, and group performance. Emphasis is on group rewards and recognition with everyone having an equal say in team activities. Communication is open and team members feel free to criticize or correct one another if needed.	Tightly connected people with an equal say within a given level but with a strong leader whose direction takes precedence over the team. Communication is downward for general work goals, and teams are usually within functional units.
	Examples: Jamaica, Argentina, Israel	Examples: South Korea, Mexico, Singapore

like Japan. It reaffirms an individual's sense of team membership and offers an important opportunity for personal growth. It is particularly effective since it provides the Japanese workers with a growth opportunity *within* a team context (growth is tied to benefits for the team). An important question asked by American managers is to what extent can these methods be adopted? Although U.S. workers may not have such a strong team identity as the Japanese, the quality circle technique may work well if it is focused on an individual's sense of growth (self-efficacy motive) and personal image (self-enhancement motive). A splendid example of the quality control emphasis used by a company is the six sigma approach of Motorola. In this company, there is a very heavy emphasis on training and empowering employees to conduct quality checks for themselves rather than relying on some external body, such as a quality control department. Thus quality control and quality products are a reflection of the personal excellence of each Motorola employee.

Summary

This chapter has been focused on the development of effective teams—their formation and maintenance. We have provided a brief background on the team as it exists in an organization as well as a general way of looking at team processes across cultures (summarized in Table 6.1). Finally, we have offered a number of applications of our model to major topics in team dynamics—conformity and creativity, team decisions, team member motivation, and the combination of teams and technological innovations.

Now that you have the tools for developing an effective team and making good decisions, how can you best lead this team? Regardless of the work to be done, the culture, or the members' motives, the key to a successful team hinges on the team leader's awareness of how to combine these elements synergistically. In the next chapter, we tackle the difficult topic of leadership in a multicultural setting.

7

Leading in Different Cultures

Perhaps no topic within the field of management excites more than that of leadership. It is a subject that has long captured the imagination of theologians, historians, and philosophers. Much of history concerns vivid descriptions of great military figures such as Alexander the Great, Julius Caesar, Joseph Stalin, and George Patton, as well as more modern corporate visionaries—Bill Gates, Lee Iacocca, and Jack Welch, Jr. We ask ourselves how these people built their empires and led their people.

In this chapter, we talk about the importance of self-knowledge to individuals and the way culture affects them. Ultimately, we believe, how well a manager's leadership style conforms to employees' self-knowledge and culture helps to determine how effective the leader is. Even better, a successful leader can understand the symbols and ideas within a culture and can take on the particular problems that confront employees. We don't mean that effective leadership focuses on people's problems—quite the opposite; effective leadership helps people face their problems and reframe them as competitive advantages. We will use our self-knowledge approach to examine the leader-subordinate(s) relationship and to show how leaders lead followers across the world. We highlight several aspects of leadership in terms of cultural values as well as describe some contradictions of leadership styles from a cultural perspective.

113

What Is a Leader?

Noel Tichy of the University of Michigan, provides a fascinating glimpse of CEO Jack Welch, Jr. of General Electric.[1] Welch who took over the reins of GE in 1981, faced a bloated, inefficient, and bureaucratic company. Within five years, Welch had transformed it in a number of striking ways, including downsizing the company, divesting inefficient business and acquiring new ones, doubling investment in research and development, and increasing returns to shareholders (and earning the title Neutron Jack in the process). The GE of the late 1980s had made a quantum change from the company Welch took control over less than a decade earlier.

Welch had a multifaceted approach to dealing with the change needed for GE. In addition to the financial and structural changes in the company, he focused attention to revamping the Crotonville Management Center used by GE to develop its executive talent. The management training center created a new way of thinking for its participants—for example, a focus on the global economy, global staffing, and development of strategic alliances. The center also moved away from a traditional emphasis on segmented learning to an integrated team approach to management problems. Welch used a combination of this new training for his top personnel as well as the structural changes to create a new environment in GE that led to his successes. What did Welch do? How did he get his employees to go along with his ideas? More importantly, would Welch's approach work at SONY of Japan or Hyundai of South Korea or Unilever of the Netherlands? The focus of this chapter lies in better understanding how a manager's leadership can transform a company and how leadership principles may be determined by culture.

Leadership is one of the most confusing terms that exists in management. It may mean power, authority, administration, control, and supervision depending on who is asked. There are many facets to leadership:

- Interactions between two or more people
- The intentional influencing of one person's actions by another person
- The energizing and directing of individuals to achieve some specified goal

One aspect of leadership is that it is an exchange between people in a way that a leader convinces a follower that the followers rewards will be improved if he follows the leaders directions. James

McGregor Burns has contrasted two very different types of leaders: *transformational* and *transactional* leaders. A transformational leader provides employees with opportunities to grow in which both leader and employees will "raise one another to higher levels of motivation and morality." A transformational leader helps to *change* a follower fundamentally. A transactional leader works by giving employees material rewards in order to get them to follow. Burns says that only the transformational leader can create a bond between a leader and an employee that remains permanent. The transactional leader can depend on his or her employees only as fair weather friends, whereas the transformational leader has loyal employees to the end.[2]

In a self-focused culture, a transformational leader can work with a follower's self-efficacy motive and provide the follower with growth opportunities. What about a transformational leader working in a group-focused culture? In this instance, to be effective she or he must focus on growth opportunities and on transformation of that group, not just a single person. A transformational leader faces a different challenge in a strong power- and status- oriented culture, such as Singapore, since the type of individual autonomy and freedom that the leader instills in a follower may contradict the expected leader-follower relationship. Employees in Singapore or India are very hesitant to take on individual responsibilities that have not been specifically provided for by a leader. A transformational leader, who empowers employees to act independently, will likely falter in a high power and status- oriented culture.

Another approach to the subject is charismatic leadership. We will elaborate on this idea later in this chapter since it provides an way of thinking about the relationship of an employee to a leader in various countries. Charismatic leaders influence the emotions, self-esteem, and self-concept of their employees. Robert House makes the distinction of transactional versus charismatic definitions when he states:

> Despite some danger of oversimplification, transactional theories describe actions of leaders that result in work behavior becoming more instrumental in employees reaching their *existing* goals while at the same time contributing to the goals of the organization. In contrast, charismatic or transformational theories address the actions of leaders that result in employees *changing* their values, goals, needs, and aspirations.[3]

A charismatic leader is someone who can energize the hearts of followers, not simply their minds. Abraham Zaleznik says that a leader determines the "right thing" to do (important to the employees as well as the organization), whereas a manager knows how to do the "right thing."[4] In other words, charismatic leaders are forward looking and visionary, but managers only carry out duties and responsibilities much in the way a technician performs a routine job.

A question that might be raised about leadership concerns a cultural bias that the leader should manipulate/guide/direct employees' reactions much as a shepherd leads a flock. This is an assumption characteristic of American thinking, though one erroneous in some cultures. The popularity of charismatic leaders in the United States reflects a cultural theme of awaiting a "savior" or "great leader." We now turn to an exploration of this question: is the charismatic leader the one preferred in all countries? What does the charismatic leader act like?

A New Way of Thinking About Leadership
Across Cultures

Our approach has three basic aspects: leader self-knowledge, subordinate self-knowledge, and cultural background and work setting. A simplified presentation of our thinking about these pieces is presented in Figure 7.1. We represent these aspects in our graphic as part of a general job situation. The cultural context refers to the society in which a company operates; the societal influence is seen in all aspects of leadership.

The ideas that we present in Figure 7.1 are an extension and elaboration of our self-knowledge approach. The relationship of a leader to an employee is determined by each person's self-concept and culture. For example, a Swedish or Norwegian leader is thought to be successful if he or she helps a work group get important rewards; the loyalty of employees to a leader hinges on the latter's helping the group grow and be rewarded. In a self-focused country like the United States, an emotional attachment can occur between a leader and subordinate. This relationship takes the form of a close friendship, and the subordinate views the leader as a source of rewards and recognition. Taking this idea one step further, the leader's and subordinate's self-knowledge helps guide the way they talk and act with one another.

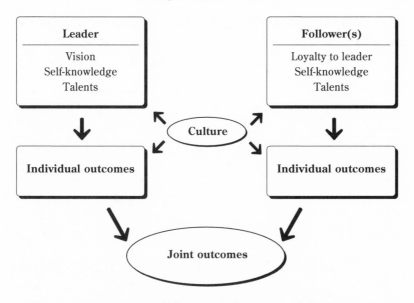

Figure 7.1 *Leadership, culture, and self-knowledge*

We also draw on the ideas of Robert Lord of the University of Akron and his colleagues in describing the way that people process their experiences about leadership.[5] Using some research from psychology, we can think about how individuals interact and how they behave in various settings according to organized patterns of ideas that people have in their memories. If we think about the cars that people drive, for example, we might also think about the specific cars that we own. We also may think about a general category of automobile as well (e.g., four wheels and an engine).

We can use this idea of a person's organized group of images in thinking about what makes an ideal leader. Who is an ideal leader, and does this collection of characteristics change from one culture to another? Without question, an American leader possesses independence, quick thinking, a take-charge approach, and a strong presence in front of others. Jack Kennedy and Lee Iacocca come immediately to mind. But what about an ideal leader in a group-focused culture such as China, or in a low -power and -status culture such as Sweden, or in a high power differential culture such as Hungary or the Czech Republic?

Sometimes these organized groups of ideas have a specific timing as well. In this case, we refer to them as scripts, much like a movie script. We mean that people's memories dictate a sequence to certain events. For instance, a new CEO succeeds a previous one who was not highly successful. What happens next? We would expect that the CEO will spend a short period getting an overview of the new company followed by the selection of key personnel as well as the reassignment or laying off others. Next we would expect the CEO to issue a general mission statement, a plan for reorganizing and refocusing the company. Finally, more specific plans and itineraries are forthcoming. What is important is that employees have this script—activities for CEO succession—and that they use it to respond to the world. When John Scully took over Apple Computer, and failed to take a strong stance or sweeping actions during the first few months of his employment, he was viewed as a weak leader by many in the computer industry, including his own employees. An example of a leader's and an employee's way of organizing ideas about culture, life experiences, general beliefs related to culture, and specific actions related to these beliefs is presented in Table 7.1. This looks at the cultural value of a group focus and its relationship to worker participation. At the level of society, there is a group focus for a leader and a follower. At the next level, we list the life experiences of work, family relationships, and friendships. Organized within this experience are the beliefs and ideas that people hold about participation—that it aids personal growth (subordinate's perspective) or that it is just and good for the company (leader's perspective). Finally, we outline the specific actions that occur as a result of those beliefs; these include a leader's decision to provide decision authority to employees and an employee's attempt to gain more influence at work.

Many aspects of a leader's or an employee's behavior can be described using these organized groups of ideas. Take, for example, Kennedy's speech about American patriotism ("Ask not what your country can do for you but what you can do for your country"). We can think about the setting for the speech, nature of presentation, and actions of leader and subordinate as working according to these organized ideas. No one attending had to be asked to remain quiet during the speech's presentation, nor did the president need to be told to use dramatic pauses to heighten emotional responses in the listeners. The content of his speech drew upon the American ideal of each person making a difference, and the dramatic pauses and emotion were ideal for inspiring Americans. At the same time, this presentation style and content may not be useful in more group-focused cultures. We are making two basic points: first, the actions of leaders and employees are not spontaneous, and their expectations guide the actions of leaders and

Table 7.1

Comparison of Leader and Subordinate Ideas About
Worker Participation in a Group-Focused Country

Category	Leader's Perspective	Subordinate's Perspective
Societal level	Group-focus—low power differential	Group-focus—low power differential
Life experiences	Work, family, friends	Work, family, friends
Beliefs and ideas about participation	Helps employee growth Just and good in society Reaffirms leader's standing in society Enhances leader's image	Reaffirms group membership Aids personal growth Provides control Signals importance
Specific actions	Speak out in favor of it Restructure jobs provide decision control to employees	Speak out in favor of it Try to gain more influence Develop good attitude toward the leader

employees; more importantly these expectations have cultural as well as personal roots.

With regard to self-knowledge, our approach emphasizes both the leader and subordinate as major actors. We believe that the actions of both are important and that they produce collective as well as individual results. Let's take as an example someone who has a high self-consistency motive (seeks continuity and stability). A leader who plunges this employee into constant turmoil and change is likely to be ineffective and resented. For the follower who has a strong need for recognition (self-enhancement), a leader must supply such attention and acknowledgement.

The final piece of our approach concerns the subtle nature of culture. We do not present this as a specific, direct cause of leader or subordinate actions. The subtle aspects of leadership reflect those things that operate between a leader and an employee, such as company structure, personal relationships, and the roles we play in our jobs. The general culture in a country indirectly affects leaders and employees through shaping the kinds of companies that exist and influencing how people work with each other in their company. For instance, Germany has a labor-management relations system called codetermination.[6] This system, mandated by national laws, provides employee participation on corporate boards as full, voting members. If a leader tries to use a different type of workplace participation, he or she will be rebuffed by employees and management alike. German law requires this unique form of workplace democracy. Now if we combine a person's self-knowledge with his or her cultural background, we can better understand how to be an effective global leader. We now turn to a discussion of the global leader.

What Makes a Successful Global Leader?

Traditional ideas about leadership emphasize traits and talents. Edwin Locke of the University of Maryland and others identified a number of traits and skills frequently associated with leadership.[7] They found that the following are important:

- Drive: achievement, ambition, and energy
- Leadership motivation: personal versus social
- Honesty and integrity
- Self-confidence and emotional stability
- Thinking and general intelligence
- Knowledge of the business
- Other traits, including charisma, flexibility, and creativity

Thus an effective leader is often thought to be adaptable, ambitious, aware of the environment, persistent, and confident. Other skills possessed by effective leaders include intelligence, creativity, organization, social skills, and persuasiveness. A generalized description of an effective leader is well represented by a quote from Ralph Stogdill:

> The leader is characterized by a strong drive for responsibility and task completion, vigor and persistence in pursuit of goals, venturesome and originality in problem solving, drive to exercise initiative in social situations, self-confidence and sense of personal identity, willingness to accept consequences of decision and action, readiness to absorb interpersonal stress, willingness to tolerate frustration and delay, ability to influence other persons' behavior, and capacity to structure social interaction systems to the purpose at hand."[8]

Do all effective leaders exhibit all of these characteristics? Certainly not. What do we find if we think of various business leaders? Sam Eichenfeld from Greyhound Financial Corporation, Bill Gates from Microsoft, and Jack Welch, Jr. from General Electric, represent three very different sets of talents, but they are all quite successful. What characteristics or talents do they share? They all have emotional stability (able to handle themselves under fire), technical skills, confidence, and a strong vision of what they wanted to accomplish. What about leaders outside of the United States? Take Y. T. Chao from the China Steel Corporation, one of the world's largest producers of steel. Y. T. Chao certainly shares these traits with the American leaders, but he has additional characteristics that reflect his Asian heritage. He also believes in using many philosophical ideas from Taoism as a spiritual guide for his leadership style. We see a strong ideological and religious orientation of Asian leaders that is often lacking in American ones. We do not imply, however, that the former are superior; merely their ideological orientation is consistent with the cultural value of spiritualism found in Asian countries.

A talent and vision-focused approach to the study of leadership has rekindled interest in the personalities of leaders and employees. This approach, discussed briefly earlier, is referred to as *charismatic leadership*. The idea of charismatic leadership comes from Max Weber who describes charismatic authority as coming from a faith in the leader's exemplary character rather than through formal rules and traditions.[9] More recent attention has focused on charisma as a personal talent or trait possessed by certain people. Robert House looked at the biographies of United States presidents to determine which were charismatic and to see if the charismatic presidents were also the effective ones. Sure enough, he found that the charismatic presidents were more likely to have created change during their administrations and to have been more popular with the public than less charismatic ones.

The idea that a charismatic leader instills a vision within employees is particularly important from a cultural perspective for a number of reasons. First, a shared vision provides employees guidance for their actions. Manfred Kets de Vries at INSEAD uses a psychoanalytic approach in his study of what makes a leader effective. He identifies underlying cultural themes that emerge as important symbols and argues that for leaders to be effective, there must be a compatibility between a leader's concerns and those faced by society.[10] In other words, a charismatic leader must make the leader's personal struggles into a shared, or universal, concern for all of the employees to solve together. Of course, a leader from one culture must use a different style in order to gain subordinate acceptance than a leader from another culture. In the United States, a business leader must struggle against the company's foes as a lone soldier. Employees must think about the leader as an "underdog" and therefore as someone who the employees will help defend. In the People's Republic of China, a leader must take care of the employees' group needs. The group-oriented leader must struggle to maintain the social well-being of a group in order that they will face challenges together. Y. T. Chao of China Steel Corporation has argued that the only way for his company to survive and excel was through the concentrated efforts of worker groups and their dedication to the company.

One of the most effective ways for charismatic leaders to transfer their personal struggles to their employees is through stories and symbols. A charismatic leader assumes the ego and conscience of the group; employees' anxieties are eased by the leader's favorable past relationships. For example, a paternalistic leader assumes the role of father figure in a society endorsing a strong and controlling relationship among parents and children, such as in Japan or South Korea.

The relationship of a charismatic's vision to cultural myths and beliefs is important since this vision is based on culture and constitutes a leader's self-knowledge. Given that culture helps shape our self-knowledge, we can see that it plays an important role for the effective leader. For example, a highly prominent managerial consultant from the United States, famous for his ability to stimulate business audiences about how to develop excellence in their organizations, uses cultural symbols and themes (heroic entrepreneurship, independence, risk taking, and so forth) in his highly motivating talks. His actions include dramatic gesturing to induce employees to become physically involved (clapping and shouting support, for example). As a charismatic leader, he uses American themes of the rugged individual; his actions demonstrate the dynamism that Americans appreciate. However, much to his surprise, he was unsuccessful when he made a lecture tour in mainland China. Why? He failed because he didn't realize that American themes and presentation were inappropriate for the Chinese. The physical and emotional outbursts that he expected are considered to be rude in Chinese culture. Managers are expected to be restrained under such circumstances as a sign of respect for the speaker.

We have focused a great deal on the leader's vision and talents, but a leader's plans for action are also crucial for success. There are three major avenues through which vision is enacted: *strategic, tactical,* and *personal.* A strategic approach refers to a clear philosophy that creates the strategic goals that shape a company. A tactical approach refers to the actual policies and programs used to operationalize a vision; these programs must involve middle- and lower-level management for them to be effective. Finally, a personal approach means focusing the attention of employees on key issues, using good communication skills, demonstrating trustworthiness, and displaying respect for workers.

A leader's actions to implement personal goals will take many forms that are consistent with more general values of employees. For instance, a leader in a self-focused culture may have personal goals that include empowering employees, giving them personal growth opportunities, and even pitting one employee against another to let the fittest survive. How would this approach work in a group-focused country? Not well at all. The self-consistency motive tells us that an effective leader will use culturally endorsed approaches with employees.

What Makes a Successful Global Follower?

Leadership can be thought of as an interesting exchange rather than simply a one-way bargain; a leader can only lead if an employee allows it. It is amazing that managers often forget this obvious truth. What is it about the subordinate's self-knowledge that creates a bond with someone?

Let's look first at the talents and loyalties of employees and how these influence a person's dedication to a leader. *Dedication* may seem like a strong word, but true leadership engenders a loyalty and commitment that can move mountains. We are not just talking about making people work harder or feel a bit more confident about their abilities. Rather, we are talking about the kind of commitment to a leader's vision that changes a person's way of thinking and living. Effective leadership requires that a leader has a strategic vision and an employee is committed to and acts on this vision. An example is McDonald's CEO Ray Kroc, who wanted his restaurants to be a place where a typical family could get an inexpensive dinner in clean and nice surroundings. Did he achieve this goal through his employees? The clear answer is yes: his employees shared his vision of the fast-food business and a willingness to take individual initiative. What about a leader such as the former CEO of Sony Corporation of Japan (group focus, high power differential)? His style was that of a benevolent father who provided groups of employees with satisfying work and the opportunity to contribute as team members toward helping the larger organization. His employees treated him with great respect, and he emphasized that everyone was working to support the Sony family.

How do an employee's talents and loyalty work through self-knowledge and culture? The self-enhancement and self-growth motives shape actions and commitment. The reader will recall that self-enhancement is a person's desire to feel good about him- or herself, and self-growth is a desire to grow and develop skills and talents. An employee's desire to grow is determined in large part by past experiences, which also determine self-image. An engineer who believes herself to be a competent mathematician will be more committed to a leader's vision of developing new computer-chip fabrication using sophisticated mathematics than an engineer who does not. The mathematically inclined engineer is attracted to such a strategic goal, whereas the other one is discouraged by such a vision. Thus a leader's ability to attract an employee depends on the subordinate's self-knowledge and desire to maintain a positive sense of self.

We can apply this thinking to the other motives of the self. Many leaders experience difficulty in overcoming employee complacency and resistance to change. This inertia is not surprising. Consistency is a natural part of everyone's self-knowledge. People are reluctant to change if they have a strong desire for consistency. This desire is not isolated from other aspects of a person's life; changes in one part of a life-style (e.g., altering work responsibilities through a job transfer) may affect continuity in other parts of the employee's life and family. Sheldon Zedeck of the University of California at Berkeley, has examined the intricate relationship of people's careers to their family and social circumstances and suggests that these are increasingly related.[11] Increasingly we need to think about an employee's life as a package that includes various pieces.

Employees' self-knowledge is influenced by other factors as well. Let's return to our comparison of a sample leader's and follower's thinking presented in Table 7.1. In our example, the subordinate shares the group-focused and low power differential values espoused within the subordinate's culture. Given these beliefs, the subordinate will generally endorse participative management practices. This attitude is supported by a number of other beliefs and feelings: participation demonstrates the employee's worth (self-enhancement), provides growth opportunities (self-growth), and so forth. These beliefs translate into types of actions . For instance, an employee may react to opportunities for participation in a number of ways—she or he may speak out in favor of it, develop a positive affect toward someone responsible for providing it, and search for ways to make effective use of it. Someone who believes in participation will likely take steps to get future occasions to participate, using such techniques as influencing a superior (or what is called upward influence).

Several conclusions can be drawn from our discussion of culture and leadership. First, we have seen that culture shapes an employee's self-knowledge Let's use the example of a group focus. in showing how it can influence an employee's beliefs. A group-focus value can directly affect people's actions (such as thinking about how to make good work decisions), or it may be related to other values and beliefs (such as thinking about good work habits or doing quality work). Therefore an effective leader realizes that the endorsement of one general value may influence various employees in very different ways.

Second, culture has an impact on the leadership process because it shapes an individual's self-knowledge. Let's take, for instance, a leader from a high-power-differential culture who is asked to manage a foreign subsidiary operating in a culture that endorses egalitarian and participative styles. The various techniques that the expatriate manager will implement are likely to fail since they are inconsistent with the employees' belief systems, sense of self, and the like. Nevertheless while one subordinate may reject the manager's authoritarian style, another may go along with it because his or her specific beliefs emphasize conformity to superiors and coworkers. In other words, we must fully understand an individual's self-knowledge and culture if we wish to be an effective leader.

Related to this second point is how employees' beliefs lead them to respond to a leader's vision. This reaction is influenced by the subordinate's beliefs about the vision, and these will vary somewhat. In fact employees' reactions to a leader's vision may be automatic or quite unpredictable. For example, one employee may routinely work longer hours as job demands require; another employee may respond by thinking of new ways to reduce waste and inefficiencies during normal work hours. Both may have accepted the leader's call for duty, but they act in very different ways based on their unique self-knowledge.

As noted earlier in the chapter, another major influence on an employee's reaction to a leader is identification with the symbols used by that individual; this can lead to identification with the leader's vision. As Manfred Kets de Vries asserts, "Employees may endow their leaders with the same magic powers and omniscience they attributed in childhood to parents or other significant figures.

Moreover, transference reactions can be acted out in different ways and may affect both leaders and employees."[12]

He suggests that transference can take one of three forms: *idealizing*, or putting the leader on an unrealistic pedestal; *mirroring*, or desiring to be the central focus of the leader's attention; and *persecuting*, or launching a vengeful attack on a leader because of feeling let down. This transference is related to the symbols and myths inherent to a culture. For example, former West Germany chancellor Helmut Kohl used a number of national beliefs and values in getting people to follow his policies. He used the image that Germany was an amalgam of many "little" people who needed a "helping hand" from the government, not a "hand out." These images tap at many aspects of German culture, including self-sufficiency, austerity, and conservatism.

Leader-subordinate relationships are influenced by a number of elements, especially a person's cultural values. An effective leader not only recognizes the relevance of common ideology, beliefs, and values but also provides opportunities for reinforcement of the subordinate's self-knowledge. Let's take, for instance, a former Southwest Airlines CEO, famous for his casual and free-wheeling interpersonal style. He set a tone for his airline that all employees were invaluable assets to the company and that the best way for a customer to enjoy their flights was for the airline attendant (service provider in their terms) also to enjoy the travel experience. Attendants would tell jokes, act familiar and friendly with passengers, pat the passengers on the back, and generally engage in friendly banter with one another. The CEO established an atmosphere of true job enjoyment (as opposed to mere job satisfaction), and his employees committed themselves to this end. This approach fits in well with the American openness willingness to be friendly with strangers. Would such an approach work for the conservative and closed culture that we find in Germany or Austria? Certainly not. It would conflict with cultural values of a closed society and norms of restraint in social action. In German culture, in-group and out-group distinctions are quite strong. It can take many years for people to become true friends. The most appropriate form of interaction, until the friendship barrier is breached, is what an American would characterize as a casual acquaintance.

Interestingly how employees feel about a leader, and why they think that the leader does certain things, influences their judgments. A tactless leader, for example, may make a faux pas and not lose standing with dedicated followers if the mistake is thought to reflect an accident rather than general incompetence. Although it's not clear how we make these judgments across cultures, it seems likely that we form them similarly in different cultures but that we rely on different sources of information. To the United States and its allies, Saddam Hussein appeared to be a megalomaniac who placed his people on the brink of disaster. To the Iraqis and Palestinians, he was a hero willing to take on seemingly insurmountable odds for the sake of a united Arab people.

What Happens If There Is Effective Leadership?

Until now, we have focused on how leaders and followers relate to one another in various cultures. We now look at the results that can be gained from the leader-subordinate relationship.

Gains from a Leader's Perspective

In many ways, probably the most important outcome for a leader is the admiration and loyalty of employees. As a leader gains favor within a group, employees reinforce the leader's position through attention, praise, admiration, and the like. These strongly reward a leader's self-knowledge through all three self-motives. For example, the administration of employees produces greater self-enhancement and a more positive self-image. The self-consistency motive is satisfied by a leader's continuing status within a group. Perhaps the most interesting aspect of a leader's personal outcomes is how an employee can shape a leader's self-efficacy. Let's say that an effective leader creates a work environment that leads to the growth of both the leader and the employees. The reinforcing value of such an environment is that the leader will take on increasingly challenging tasks and persist until they are accomplished. The leader is then more likely to continue being successful, and this result fuels even more success. As Ray Kroc says, nothing is more important than hard work and persistence. In his office, Kroc had the following message posted as a reminder:

> Nothing in the world can take the place of persistence.
> Talent will not; nothing is more common than unsuccessful men with great talent.
> Genius will not; unrewarded genius is almost a proverb.
> Education will not; the world is full of educated derelicts.
> Persistence, determination alone are omnipotent.[13]

Thus leaders who challenge both themselves and their followers will receive employee support, and they are more likely to develop more challenges for themselves leading to even greater successes and admiration.

There is an additional, personal reward that leaders can receive. Remember, effective leaders use their bond with their employees to project their problems onto the followers. The use of projection not only commits employees to solving problems but also provides leaders with an *outlet* for their own problems. We should not overlook the relevance of self-purging as an outcome, as well as a motive, for given leadership actions. Leaders who desire to assert themselves as paternal figures will use an authoritarian leadership context as a way of satisfying self-concept struggles. At the same time, we can see a potential problem with this procedure if the culture does not approve of this projection.

Gains from an Employee's Perspective

Employees obviously gain from good leadership as well. They will get opportunities to contribute, to challenge themselves, and to receive evaluations that build their sense of self-efficacy. Effective leaders identify employees' weaknesses and strengths and give them support and structure, so the employees can avoid failures and attain confidence-building successes. Of course, for employees from group-focused cultures, like the Czech Republic or Taiwan, personal growth opportunities must not come at the expense of group welfare; an individual there can grow by helping the group.

Effective leaders work with their employees to give them work assignments that reflect well on their self-image. Successful leaders recognize the important facets of the lives of employees and give them ample opportunity to succeed in these areas. Such an approach sounds tough, since it implies that work opportunities must be tailored to each employee, but leaders may rely on a cultural approach to choose these opportunities.

Finally, we can talk about an employee's rewards and self-consistency. Kets de Vries suggests that the transference process provides employees with a powerful way to confront their own these problems and resolve them. Many individuals, particularly in stressful circumstances, transfer these problems to their leaders. People who have a strong desire for consistency may treat their leader as a parent figure; as authority figures, leaders provide an ideal outlet for unresolved tension. An employee may endow the leader with special qualities that can help to resolve these personal problems.

An important joint outcome of leader-subordinate exchange is mutual growth, or what might be called a group growth. Just as individuals learn and grow, so do groups. The exchange of ideas and development of mutual goals provide the foundation for a group of people to develop a sense of special identity. The Apple Macintosh development team, for example, had a vision of a new computer system interface, but it had to build on various team members' strengths in order to develop the new system collectively. The group used varied talents and developed a joint purpose and interpersonal relationships to fulfill a mutual goal.

Along with the relationships and commitments of the Macintosh team came a social hierarchy, shared history (albeit short term), and rules and norms. Once the members were together, they had to decide what role each person would play (evolving from existing roles), how to relate to their group leader, what attachments they would form to one another, and how new members joining the team as time passed would be initiated. Although many of these issues are heavily influenced by existing social rules and practices, each group will develop its own unique form as it evolves. Thus group growth refers to the resulting patterns and rules that emerge as leaders and employees work together.

Other Influences

A final part of our discussion concerns a few events that can have an impact on the leader-follower relationship. First, leaders and employees often work together in an organization that itself is shaped by culture. For example, manufacturing companies in Russia are often bureaucratic and hierarchical. In the United States, companies are often decentralized and less hierarchical. These differences influence how a leader and subordinate interact. In a highly bureaucratic organization, a leader is quite far removed from his or her employees. If this type of company is exported to a culture that stresses equality, problems of leader-subordinate communication obviously may occur.

Another factor affecting the leader-subordinate relationship is the roles that people play. These dictate the ways that leaders and employees can talk with each other. For example, the Japanese (as do the Koreans) consider it inappropriate for an employee to criticize a superior during work. Yet it is not only acceptable but expected that such criticisms will be voiced after working hours when the superior and employees go to dinner or have drinks. Their view is that the roles enacted by the superior and employees are fundamentally different during the evening than during the daytime. Further, it is expected that the superior listen to the criticism but not acknowledge it the next day during work.

Table 7.2

Summary of Effective Leadership Style in Various Cultures

	Low Power Differential	High Power Differential
Self-focused	Leader comes from among the rank and file, and he/she is careful not to act better than or different from followers. He/she addresses followers' needs and wants by matching them to those of the leader so the burden of leadership is shared. The leader treats all followers as individuals and can differentially reward people as long as it is justified. The leader is seen as a unique person but one who cannot forget that he/she came from average people.	Leader can come from among the rank and file but often is from a special class or group, such as a more educated group, or upper-class family. The leader maintains a distance between the follower and the leader, and he/she emphasizes the need for the leader's problems to be those important to the follower. The leader is "larger than life," and it is important that he/she remains aloof from individual followers while treating them as individuals.
	Examples: United States, New Zealand, Finland	Examples: South Africa, Italy, Spain
Group-focused	Leader comes from among the dominant work group and has his/her strongest connection with the dominant work coalition. In some cases, the leadership is rotated among different group members as well. The emphasis is not on the leader as a unique person but on a facilitator, who can help the work group achieve important outcomes. Followers identify with the leader's views and ideas as much as the leader him- or herself.	Leader comes from the dominant group in a company, and this position is often gained through family or personal contacts. The leader is viewed as all-powerful and must treat all group members comparably. Individual followers are kept at a distance, and the emphasis is placed on dealing with groups of employees and leading these groups as intact units rather than as unique individuals. An emphasis is placed on rank and position in which a leader's status is maintained by keeping subordinates in their position.
	Examples: Jamaica, Argentina, Israel, and Sweden	Examples: South Korea, Mexico, Singapore, and Saudi Arabia

Roles also reinforce our "ideal" of how to act. An American cultural bias that is built into much of the work on charismatic leadership is that a leader is a risk taker. This romantic view is consistent with Western thinking, but it doesn't necessarily work elsewhere. In countries like Japan, Greece, and Portugal, risk taking is not admired; it is seen as foolishness. In this sense, a charismatic leader is restricted to particular kinds of roles that are endorsed by the leader's culture.

Summary

Our purpose in this chapter has been to show how our approach of self-knowledge can be used to understand leadership across countries and cultures. We have looked at a number of examples of great leadership, including GE's Jack Welch, Jr., China Steel's Y. T. Chao, and Microsoft's Bill Gates, and described it in terms of the leaders' and the followers' self-knowledge and culture. We summarize the various characteristics of leaders from a variety of cultures and countries in Table 7.2.

How leaders work with their employees is shaped by the practices used in their companies, and these are affected by the culture in which they operate. For example, in the decentralized companies of Sweden or in the Israeli kibbutz, a leader's effectiveness will be improved if that individual relies on face-to-face talks to win people over. At the same time an authoritarian leader who wishes to order people about in such a low -power and -status culture is likely to become frustrated.

Moreover, the roles of leader and subordinate are strongly influenced by the way people in a country generally operate. How many times have you heard troubling stories of women expatriate managers who work in male-dominated countries? Judy Rosener has written an interesting book about the roles and problems of women managers in an international work force: she suggests that women are a relatively untapped resource in most industrialized nations. The ways that people interact in different cultures are based on the expectations of leaders and followers alike.

Even though a leader's employees may be highly motivated and dedicated, the creation of quality products is no longer a simple challenge of getting people to "try harder." We now turn our attention to a serious challenge for every leader: namely, how to develop quality products as people work.

8

Quality and the Committed Worker

Total quality management (TQM) has become a focus of interest for managers around the world in almost the full range of industrial sectors, from manufacturing to service, health care, education, and government. While the success of TQM in Japan has been widely documented, a McKinsey study in Europe and the United states found that two thirds of quality improvement programs have failed to show the expected results. The focus of this chapter will be to answer the following questions: why do quality improvement (QI) programs succeed in some cultures and fail in others, and how can managers across the world cope with the need to improve quality? If we apply our approach of *cultural self-knowledge* approach to answer these questions, we find that quality improvement programs sometimes fail because not enough attention is given to their meaning by the employees who implement them and not enough care is given to select implementation strategies appropriate to the given culture. In this chapter, we will define the role of self-knowledge for understanding the typical reaction people have to quality improvement programs. We also propose the 3-D model of QI, which consists of the implementation of QI on three levels (the individual, the group, and the organization) and adjusts the emphasis given to each level in line with cultural characteristics. Finally, we examine the potential success of QI throughout the world and suggest appropriate strategies for implementation of quality improvement programs in various cultures.

The Role of Self-Knowledge

Quality improvement is a process of continuous change. This reality may create problems in implementing QI for at least two reasons. First, as already noted, change seems to violate the motive of self-consistency. Nevertheless, continuous change that leads to the fulfillment of self-motives *is* consistent with peoples' needs, therefore this type of change actually does not violate the self-consistency motive. Second, people commonly react with suspicion and fear to imposed changes. Change in the work environment often creates discomfort and tension because its outcomes are typically unknown. People tend to be averse to risk, preferring the status quo to an uncertain though possibly better outcome. Continuous improvement requires an ongoing adaptation of attitudes, skills, and behavior.

To adapt to new situations, people need to assess new demands and what they must do to cope with those requirements effectively. People want to know why change is needed before they are willing to take action; they become motivated to facilitate change after they develop self-knowledge, discover how to interpret change, and determine the meaning of its consequences for their well-being and self-worth. Individuals are more likely to endorse change when it brings opportunities for satisfying their needs for self-enhancement and self-growth. Therefore, to successfully implement QI programs, you should help your subordinates develop self-knowledge and vision (or foresight) of how the change will benefit them as well as the organization. The development of self-knowledge, as previously indicated, involves the following steps:

1. Determine the relative strength of your own self-motives and those of your subordinates.

2. Determine the type of culture you come from and that of your subordinates (e.g., high or low power differential and group or self-focus).

3. Work on diversifying your self-motives and those you share with your subordinates.

4. Examine how quality improvement suits your motives and culture as well those of your subordinates.

5. Modify the approach you take to fit both your own culture and motives and those of your subordinates.

These five steps provide the foundation necessary for successful quality improvement.

To illustrate how self-knowledge can be developed within the QI programs, we turn our focus to principles outlined by one of the founders of quality improvement, Edward Deming.[1] Deming's philosophy was widely accepted in Japan and led to a revolution in the quality of Japanese products and services. His principles of quality improvement advocate self-knowledge and a continuous learning process, which makes employees feel capable and good about themselves.

For example, the principle that advocates consistency of purpose toward improvement of products and services clarifies the meaning of quality improvement to the individual. Unfolding the intrinsic motive for improving quality also helps to create a vision of where change will lead and explains the rationale for implementing the QI program. Further, the principle of adopting quality improvement as a philosophy of life, rather than just a technique, adds value and meaning that fulfill self-enhancement motives.

In addition, Deming calls for the removal of barriers that rob hourly workers of their right to pride of workmanship. Pride at work satisfies employees' needs for self-enhancement. Deming also argues that education and self-improvement are essential to the success of QI. Education promotes change by equipping people with knowledge and skills that allow them to deal with change effectively instead of fearing and resisting it. Education and communication also help employees to become motivated to implement change. Employees cannot be expected to be motivated to improve quality when they do not have the necessary knowledge and skills to do it. Transformation through education was further stressed by Ishikawa, who coined the axiom "Quality begins with education and ends with education."

While Deming's principles can be used in a general way to develop QI programs, they do not directly address how to implement these across cultures to satisfy individual self-motives for consistency, growth, and enhancement. In Chapter 3, we proposed that because cultures vary in their self- versus-group focus, the source of evaluation used in the workplace is important. To implement QI programs successfully, care must be given to sources used, and which source is given the most credence is influenced by cultural values.

People in self-focused countries like Britain and Australia use self-evaluation to determine whether quality improvement makes them feel competent, capable, and good about themselves. This situation suggests that implementation of quality programs in those cultures should allow for a focus on individual contribution as well as evaluation. By contrast, employees in group-focused cultures like Korea and China in the Far East, Mexico and Venezuela in the Americas, and Turkey in the Middle East use groups as a source of evaluation. Their self-evaluation is influenced by being part of a successful group and by getting positive evaluation from others. Therefore, in group-focused cultures, QI programs should primarily be implemented at the team level.

Managers who grew up in one culture but work in a foreign country often fall prey to using their own sources of evaluation and overlooking the those used in their host country. These managers must learn about the self-motives of their employees for enhancement, growth, and consistency and must identify the source of their evaluation of the QI program.

A General Model for Implementing Quality Improvement: The 3-D Model

The 3-D model of quality improvement states that an effective program should be implemented on three levels: organizational, team, and individual. The implementation of quality improvement on the organizational level enhances commitment of top level management and creates the infrastructure necessary for a good program. The team level is often where most of the activities of quality improvement take place. Yet all teams consist of individuals who should feel personally responsible for quality improvement thus rewarding both team and individual efforts strengthen the effectiveness of the QI program. The 3-D model provides a framework for implementing QI programs that can be modified to fit the particular cultural characteristics of the work environment. For example, in cultures with high power differential, top management should take the ultimate responsibility for the process of implementation, whereas in cultures with low power differential, top management should share the responsibility by empowering employees and/or utilizing self-management teams. Furthermore, the model suggests QI program implementation strategies for each of the three levels according to the emphasis given to the level in the culture. Figure 8.1 presents the 3-D model of quality improvement.

The Organizational Level

MANAGEMENT INVOLVEMENT

This component is a key factor in the successful implementation of any program. Upper management must be personally involved in

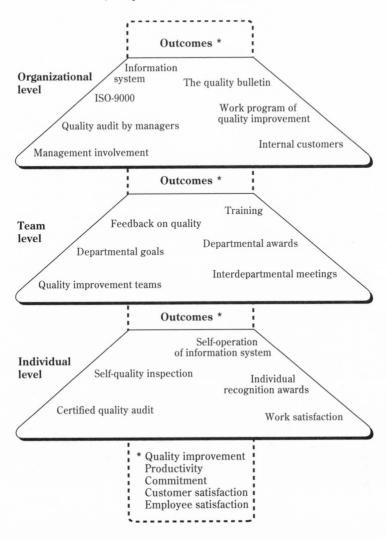

Figure 8.1 *The 3-D model of quality improvement in practice*

and committed to the strategic development of the program. In essence upper management should serve as the role model for QI. Managers may show their support by sponsoring companywide, program-related activities, including the development of information system for data collection, the implementation of training programs, on-sight visits, and awards to employees for remarkable achievements in quality improvement. In addition, communicating the vision of quality improvement can be achieved through activities such as issuing quality bulletins, writing articles, and making oral presentations. The role of the leader in quality improvement is universal, and it is equally important in all cultures.

QUALITY AUDIT BY MANAGERS

Managers must introduce QI as part of their role at all organizational levels, not as a separate function. Senior managers may serve as quality auditors and assess the level of quality improvement. Immediate managers can take on the role of team leaders, and direct the day-to-day activities, as well as team meetings for quality improvement. Involvement by all managerial levels is necessary in all cultures.

ISO-9000

ISO-9000 is the standard for quality management for manufacturers, issued by The International Organization for Standardization.[2] ISO-9000 has been accepted by all the national standards bodies, and qualification to sell across national boundaries is supported by ISO-9000 certification. ISO-9000 is a standard for quality management systems that involves not only technical aspects of manufacturing (product standards, calibration, and measurement) but also the overall management system for ensuring the continued operation necessary for improving quality. The quality management system consists of the following elements: policy and organization, design and change control, procurement, production, inspection and testing, calibration and measurement, finished goods and shipping, audits, training, and housekeeping. Registration as an ISO-9000 company is granted on the basis of quality manual assessment and on-sight inspection by a certification agency. As the international standard, ISO-9000 should be incorporated into any quality improvement process. Organizations in the service sector can also gain by following many of the ideas set forth by ISO-9000 guidelines.

INFORMATION SYSTEM

Managing by facts is a universal characteristic of QI. In order to manage by facts, it is necessary to design, develop, and install an information system that facilitates the collection of data on performance measures, the production of figures, and the provision of feedback in real time. For example, the information system may consist of quantitative measures such as the percentage of defects, machine downtime, preventive maintenance, total working hours, and the cost of quality. Measures can be aggregated at various levels (individual, departmental, etc.) and for various time periods (shifts, days, weeks). The information system allows an organization continuously to monitor performance quality, provide continuous feedback, and, consequently, improve performance quality.

The development of an information system that allows for data collection and analysis is necessary for the successful implementation of TQM across cultures.

COMMUNICATION

A bulletin can serve to communicate information concerning quality-related issues. For example, a message from the CEO, recognition of the quality person of the month, and ideas developed and implemented by quality improvement teams can be published monthly in a special quality improvement bulletin. In-house broadcasts and electronic mail from top-level executives can also be used to contact employees "personally" throughout the organization. Written and oral communication is important in any culture; however, its content and style of communication may vary across cultures.

WORK PROGRAM OF QUALITY IMPROVEMENT

This is the "how-to" program that lists and describes all the activities in the project. In group-focused cultures, this program is geared toward teamwork, and it involves the training of team leaders, the training of team members, the setting of group goals, the provision of feedback on group performance, and the like. In self-focused cultures, this program may include the aforementioned items but should also include issues surrounding the improvement of personal quality.

CHAIN OF INTERNAL CUSTOMERS

The formation of a chain of internal customers also serves to implement quality improvement in the organization. According to this approach, each department serves as the customer of other departments. Departments that provide services to others aim at obtaining customer satisfaction by meeting deadlines and budget constraints and by providing high-quality service and products. The success of any quality improvement program is evaluated by customer satisfaction. Therefore the chain of internal customers should be part of any quality improvement program.

WORK SATISFACTION

This is highly valued in organizational systems that emphasize the human resource. Satisfied employees are more willing to focus attention on quality-related issues and to improve their performance quality. For this reason a company's goal to improve quality should be accompanied by the goal to enhance its employee level of satisfaction. This can be monitored through periodic employee surveys to assess attitudes such as commitment and satisfaction.

The Team Level

QUALITY IMPROVEMENT TEAMS

The purpose of the QI teams is not only to avoid defects but also to be innovative, to develop new work methods and processes that reduce the cost of quality, and to improve the products and services. Teams can be formed in small groups (five to ten) workers who share the same or similar work responsibilities. If the teams preexisted the quality program, they can undertake responsibility for QI. If the work was designed for individual employees, new teams should be formed to undertake the QI program. Regular meetings should be held for purposes like analyzing performance feedback, solving problems, setting quality goals, and participating in training courses to improve the teams' knowledge, skills, and methods. The team leaders should be trained in how to run effective meetings and how to develop team work and group cohesiveness, as well as how to improve quality.

DEPARTMENTAL GOALS

Given their power as a motivational technique, periodic goals are an effective tool to achieve continuous improvement. Recall that goals may be set at a team and/or an individual level and may be assigned or set participatively. The most effective method will depend on the predominant culture, as well as the organization of work.

FEEDBACK ON QUALITY

Feedback is considered to be a strong motivational tool. The data gathered by the information system can be processed to produce valuable feedback for employees and work teams. This may take various forms with the intention of conveying changes in performance quality. For example, graphs may be posted in each work area, displaying weekly and monthly performance relative to the goal. Again, depending on the culture and nature of performance, feedback may be most effective on a group or individual level.

TRAINING

The purpose of training should be threefold: to internalize the values of quality improvement; to improve the statistical knowledge and technical skills necessary to interpret quality measures and to take corrective actions; and to improve group problem solving, morale, and group cohesiveness. Of course, emphasis can be shifted from groups to individuals to correspond to job requirements.

QUALITY AWARDS

This activity aims at increasing the level of both motivation and commitment to quality improvement by offering special recognition awards to either groups or individuals, depending on the cultural emphasis.

INTERDEPARTMENTAL MEETINGS

These meetings facilitate the flow of communication in the chain of internal customers. They serve to get feedback from internal customers, to identify problems, and to develop joint suggestions for improvement. Input from internal customers initiates the process of quality improvement.

The Individual Level

CERTIFIED QUALITY AUDIT

A certification program can be developed to accredit employees who have excelled at their job and have acquired theoretical and practical knowledge to become certified auditors.

SELF QUALITY INSPECTION

Employees can be trained to use tools and measures necessary for self-inspection. Self-inspection serves as a form of empowerment and grants employees a high level of personal responsibility. As a result, employees are more motivated to improve quality.

SELF OPERATION

The self-operation of the information system is another way for developing quality-related skills. Employees who are trained to operate the information system know how to collect the data, to feed it into the computer, to use statistical programs for analyzing the data, and to get computer output in the form of tables and graphs.

PERSONAL FEEDBACK

In addition to feedback on the team level, employees may receive personal feedback on how well they performed as individuals relative to quality goals and to previous periods. Personal feedback enables employees to improve personally and to contribute to their team performance.

PERSONAL RECOGNITION AWARDS
These serve for motivating individual employees and for rewarding individual contribution to quality improvement.

In addition to the just mentioned individual components, a self-focused work environment may also suggest certain team-level components (goals, feedback, rewards) more appropriate to implementation at the individual level.

Selecting 3-D Implementation Strategies that Accord with Culture

The components just described can be utilized to effectively implement QI programs in any culture, providing emphasis and sources of evaluation are aligned to the self-motives of work force. The four predominant cultural types (e.g., self- versus group focus and high versus low power differential) must be considered in order to implement the 3-D model effectively. It is our belief that these organizational components should receive equal emphasis regardless of culture. They serve as the backbone to a QI program, create vision, and cultivate commitment throughout the organization. However, the process of decision making will vary based on culture, QI programs in low-power-difference cultures allow for decision making at lower levels in the organization, whereas employees in high-power-difference cultures will expect and react favorably to decisions made from above. In addition, the relative emphasis on the team versus the individual should be adjusted according to culture.

In countries with a low power differential and a self-focus (Australia, the United Kingdom, and the North American countries, for example), an ideal QI program empowers employees and gives them autonomy and responsibility for quality improvement. In countries with a self-focus but a high power differential (for instance, France, Belgium, and Italy), effective QI programs are targeted at the individual level, as in the previous group of countries, but their top executives take more control and provide more guidance than in countries with low power differential.

In countries with a group focus and a low power differential (Norway, Sweden, Denmark, and Israel), top-management teams should initiate the program but delegate the responsibility to self-managed teams held responsible for quality improvement by emphasizing team performance and problem solving. These teams need feedback on team-level performance and quality improvement, which should be rewarded and recognized. To carry out their mission successfully, teams also need training to develop interpersonal skills, interpersonal communication, and effective teamwork.

In cultures with a group focus but a high power differential (the Far East, India, the Middle East, and South America), top-management teams need to endorse and direct quality improvement programs. In these cultures, QI programs should be created at the team level, as in the previous group of countries. However, unlike the two previously described groups of countries, top-level management must be more authoritative in the implementation of QI programs. In countries with a high power differential, employees need and expect more direction and control from their management.

QI programs created and implemented according to the guidelines for each of the four types of cultures described in this chapter will be well received by employees, because they create opportunities for the fulfillment of the self-motives of enhancement, growth, and consistency, each of which is shaped by culture. As a result, these programs will motivate employees and lead to quality improvement and the strengthening of the corporate competitive advantage.

Quality Improvement Around the World

Now we will explore QI programs around the world, some successful and some not. We examine elements of the programs in the light of the 3-D model in order to explain these outcomes. We will begin with illustrating how the 3-D model was implemented in Israel, Japan, the United States, and Britain.

QI in Israel

A successful QI program was implemented in an Israeli manufacturing firm that maintains and repairs mechanical parts of vehicles. Because of the group-focused, low power differential culture, interventions were primarily targeted at the organizationwide and team levels. At the organization level, the top-management team was actively involved with the development of policies and strategies. ISO-9000 was an integral part of the strategic program, and an information system was in place to measure key variables relating to the cost of quality. Training programs were developed, as was a work program—the "how to" program of teamwork, team training, team goals, and feedback on team performance. Quality bulletins were also distributed throughout the organization monthly. Further, the organization was restructured to take the form of a chain of internal customers.

At the team level, shop-floor employees (working in twenty-eight functional teams that consisted of five to ten employees) assumed responsibility for QI. Projects goals were set on the team level. Each month, the teams gathered together to set new goals for the following month on the basis of the performance feedback, and to discuss strategies for improvement. On an individual level, employees were given personal feedback and trained to use the information system to collect and process quality data. In addition, a program to certify employees as quality auditors was initiated, as well a quality award for individual contribution. Israel does have a group focus, but it is not as strong as in some other countries (e.g., Japan); thus some evaluation on the individual level seemed necessary.

The project started in September 1993, and it is continuing today. Quality outcomes for the first twenty-two months of the project reveal it to be highly effective. First, an external evaluation showed the plant had increased enough to accredit the plant for ISO-9000. As shown in Figure 8.2 there was dramatic improvement in the level of quality. The cost of higher quality dropped from 22 percent to 2 percent. It should be noted that the incentive pay in the company was based on the number of nondefect products. Therefore, when the level of quality improved, employees produced more quality products, they invested less time in repairs, and they got higher incentives.

Inventory costs decreased by 11 percent. Cost savings, as a result of an employee suggestions system, were four times higher at the end of data collection than prior to the implementation of QI. The accident rate decreased by 62 percent. There was also a significant change in the organizational culture: survey measures of unit emphasis on quality, innovation, attention to details, and team orientation and supportiveness increased significantly. In addition, employees expressed a high level of commitment to the quality improvement program and a relatively high level of work satisfaction.

Success of this program is largely attributable to the appropriate implementation strategies selected on the basis of the cultural characteristics of the Israeli culture. QI programs targeted the entire organization and stressed the participation and involvement

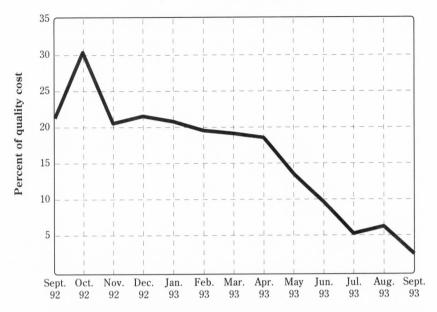

Figure 8.2 *The trend of quality cost in thirteen months*

of all employees. Work teams were given training, responsibility, feedback, rewards, and recognition for performance gains, an approach suitable to the group evaluation criteria used by Israelis.

An additional component of this project was to examine the relative effect of the following four 3-D components on both employee attitudes and performance criteria: (1) ISO-9000; (2) the work program of quality improvement, which consisted of the development of quality measures, the collection and analysis of performance quality, team development and training, feedback, and team problem solving; (3) the message from top-level management emphasizing the value of quality; and (4) quality improvement goals set on the team level. To determine their impact, the four factors were introduced across departments in a staggered manner over time, with cost of quality (measured by the percentage of work hours spent on the repair of rejects out of the total work hours) as well as attitudes and values (assessed by the departments' commitment to the project and work satisfaction) taken at four, four-month intervals.

When ISO-9000 (the technical factor) was implemented by itself, the level of work satisfaction decreased significantly. This finding suggests that employees resent new technical requirements if they do not get any additional message from top management that stresses the importance of quality improvement, as well as a work program and the necessary training to implement QI. The results of the project lead to two major recommendations:

1. ISO-9000, the technical factor, should not be implemented by itself. Rather, it should be supported by the message from top management and by a work program.

2. Time plays an important role in the process of internalization of the culture of quality. Both the cultural values and the level of performance quality improved with the length of exposure and practice. Therefore the outcomes of a quality improvement program should be tested after at least one year of implementation.

We view these recommendations as universal. ISO-9000 standards suggest mechanistic changes to organizations. QI programs are likely to fail without also focusing on human resource strategies to equip and motivate the people who are expected to create quality products. These strategies should include interventions that develop the knowledge and skills needed to implement QI, followed by goals that direct attention toward quality. These areas are at least as important as the technical aspects of any QI program. While group-focused cultures (like Israel) will benefit most by implementing this on a group level, more self-focused cultures may find focusing on the individual level to be most effective. Patience is also a virtue in QI programs. Organizations often expect immediate return on their investment in quality; yet studies reveal these returns often take three years to develop.

QI Programs in Japan

Some of the most successful QI programs have been implemented in Japan. The effectiveness of these is largely due to how Japanese firms have aligned QI strategies with their group-focused, high-power-distance culture. In this type of culture, direction and control over QI decisions should come from superiors. In terms of the 3-D model, Japan's approach to QI focuses on both the organizational and team levels, with a small focus on the individual level.

Quality improvement in Japan begins at the organizational level with the attitudes and behaviors of top-level executives. For them, quality improvement is a philosophy of management and becomes a means to show their competitiveness, to increase their company's market share, to be part of a strong company, and to have their company be part of a successful country. Top executives thus take direct responsibility for quality issues. They visit factories, branches, and offices in person to evaluate and diagnose quality control on the spot and to conduct quality control's diagnosis and auditing. They personally deal with customers complaints, as seen in the following example. A European company in the aviation industry ordered some electronic parts from a Japanese company. When the parts arrived, they could not be assembled into the final product. They called the company in Japan, and the representative of the company promised to send a technical team to Europe to help solve the problem. Two days later, the Japanese team arrived, accompanied by one of the top executives who worked with the team to solve the problem. The parts were fixed in a couple of days, and the team left. The example demonstrates that Japanese top executives take personal responsibility for quality improvement, and they motivate their employees by serving as role models. This case exemplifies the high power differential: superiors take control and give direction.

Japanese firms by and large advocate continuous quality improvement. For this purpose, they develop specific quality criteria and an extensive quality tracking system. The Japanese have also adopted the philosophy that quality improvement should be companywide, and all employees are responsible.

In line with their group culture, Japanese QI programs are designed for teams. As noted in Chapter 4, Japanese organizations place priority on the continuity and prosperity of the organization as a whole—a tendency that has been labeled *groupism* by Kunio Odaka of Tokyo University.[3] This value emphasizes close-knit relationships exemplified by the system of lifetime employment, group harmony and cooperation, participative management, and duty, and devotion and responsibility toward the particular closed group found in Japan. Groupism supports the infrastructure for team building, employee participation in quality improvement, and integration across organizational units. The cultural characteristics of groupism and close relationships have led to the development of a managerial philosophy known as management familism because it follows the strong family relationships and the mutual commitment of family members. This paternalistic approach to work relationships can be explained in light of the country's high power distance. It is also interesting to note that quality programs in Japan do not result in removing levels of management. Firms remain quite hierarchical in structure, a fact that can also be explained by the high power distance found in Japan.

We have already discussed Japanese quality control circles (QCs). The basic philosophy of QCs is to contribute to the development and improvement of the organizational system. From the employee's perspective, this system allows everyone to participate and to have the opportunity to experience enhancement and efficacy as part of the group. QCs encompass all the organizational levels, from top to bottom, and they are both hierarchical and lateral. Through participation in QCs, employees have successfully identified significant problems and created solutions to these. QCs address a variety of topics: general quality improvement, cost issues, efficiency, safety, errors, equipment, morale, control, and ways to operate the circle. In line with Japan's high power distance, a group leader is appointed to each QC. This person receives extensive training in quality and team management and runs these regular meetings.

Japanese organizations also utilize interdepartmental teams. These are formed to facilitate communication and problem solving. The emphasis placed on QI at the team level can not be understated. In fact, one of the few individual-level components of QI in Japan are suggestion systems (described in Chapter 4).

Quality improvement activities on the company level are supported by the nationwide organization of the QI Circle Headquarters at the Japanese Union of Scientists and Engineers. This organization provides information on how to start up the quality control circles activities, how to operate them, and how to maintain and reassure their continuation. The organization established the national Deming prize awarded to companies that have attained remarkable results in quality improvement.

Japanese-style QI programs can be adapted in other cultures where self-knowledge and a sense of well-being are influenced by group evaluation. Of course, the same programs are not suitable for people in self-focused cultures. Indeed, in contrast to Japan, quality control circles are not popular in the United States. A 1992 survey conducted by Edward Lawler, Susan Mohrman, and Gerald Ledford of Fortune 1,000 companies revealed that 70 percent of the companies reported that almost none of their employees were involved in QC type programs, and only 2 percent of the companies reported that 80 percent or more of their workforce were involved in quality circles. Overall quality control circles did not have a strong impact on quality improvement in the United States Lawler et al. concluded: "Quality circles are seen as less successful than survey feedback and participation groups.... They may not be a good long-term approach to employee involvement. In addition, during the middle 1980s, quality circles became a fad, and it is possible that some of the drop in their success rating is due to overuse and misuse."[4]

QI in the United States

The lack of success of QCs in the United States can be explained by its stronger focus on private evaluation and personal standards: membership in a successful group does not alone satisfy self-motives. This emphasis on making quality a personal issue is captured by Roberts and Sergesketter. "Quality is a very personal obligation. If you can't talk about quality in the first person then you have not moved to the level of involvement of quality that is absolutely essential.... You must be a believer that quality is a very personal responsibility."[5]

These researchers recommend using a simple, individual level tool that they call personal quality checklist, which quickly improves general work effectiveness and quality. They claim that the personal quality checklist has greatly improved the effectiveness of meetings in the central region of AT&T and aided in systematic quality training there. To begin a personal quality checklist, one simply has to keep track of shortcomings or defects and of cycle time. The aim is to reduce both defects and cycle time for important personal processes. The idea is to write a checklist that

Personal quality checklist: week of _____

Defect Category	Mon.	Tue.	Wed.	Thu.	Fri.	Sat.	Sun.	Total
Late for meeting or appointment								
Search for something misplaced or lost								
Delayed return of phone call or reply to letter								
Putting a small task in a "hold pile"								
Failure to discard incoming junk promptly								
Missing a chance to clean up junk in office								
Unnecessary inspection								
Total								
Comments								

Figure 8.3 *Example of personal quality checklist*

conveys all of the activities that should be done at work. A typical checklist is presented in Figure 8.3.

The list would record such information as tardiness for meetings, search for something misplaced or lost, or the delayed return of phone calls or reply to letters. Roberts and Sergesketter argue that the checklist promotes awareness, costs almost nothing, and yields accurate, real-time data on one's personal work. Each stroke is an opportunity to think about possible improvements. the personal quality checklist is a generic tool that can be adapted to different types of work.

Although personal quality is necessary, (and self-focused cultures encourage improvement of quality on a personal basis) it is not enough to implement a companywide program in a complex organization effectively. At this level, a system approach—including organizational, team, and individual strategies—is necessary to make QI successful. The national U.S. initiative to reward quality improvement systems, rather than individuals, has been led by the creation of the Malcolm Baldridge National Quality Award, established in 1987. The award recognizes firms that have achieved excellence through adherence to the quality improvement process.

Among the winners since 1987 are Motorola, Federal Express, Xerox Business Products and System Group, General Motors Cadillac Division, IBM-Rochester, and the Wallace Company. Blackburn and Rosen have identified that winners of the National Quality Award in the United States implemented a set of policies and strategies for human resource management that helped them achieve quality improvement gains.[6] At organizational, team, and individual levels, these policies and strategies were implemented in seven different areas: communication, job design, training, evaluation systems, reward systems, career development and health and safety.

COMMUNICATION

At the organizational level, each Baldridge winner has established a corporate vision to pursue TQM culture and developed strategies for communicating the vision throughout the organization. The cultural shift toward TQM requires top management to open communication with employees and to "walk the talk," as they say at Xerox. Companies like Federal Express, Cadillac, and IBM-Rochester use a variety of means for communication, including in-house television networks, company papers, and face-to-face meetings on important quality topics. In addition, all Baldridge Award winners encourage employee voice and involvement. These systems are both team and individually focused and include: round-table meetings, open-door policies, suggestion systems, advisory groups, task forces, and cross-functional teams to make suggestions and solve problems. On an individual level, employees are delegated power and authority. In addition, attitude surveys monitor employee satisfaction and identify problem areas. The results are fed back to the managerial levels, and managers are asked to address employee concerns.

JOB DESIGN

Individual jobs are often combined into cross-functional work teams that can operate permanently or on an ad hoc basis to deal with quality problems. Cross-functional teams increase the interdependence of teams and the need to work with others rather than as independent individuals; thus the team approach can be implemented more effectively even in a self-focused culture. Job design in the form of task interdependence increases the level of cooperation; cooperation and collective responsibility are further enhanced by shifting the focus from the job to the organization. Jobs can be redesigned to grant employees more authority and responsibility than they had in the past. For example, customer service is improved when employees have more discretion in making decisions and do not have to get time-consuming approvals. Japanese managers show support through participation, whereas American managers use *empowerment.* Henk Sims and Peter Lorenzi define empowerment as the act of strengthening a person's belief in his or her sense of effectiveness.[7] Frequently empowerment is identified as a form of delegation, which is the equivalent of employee participation in Japan.

TRAINING

Training is crucial for the acquisition of knowledge and skills and for the internalization of values and norms of behavior. The quality award winners invest in training more than other companies. Training is not inexpensive. For example, Cadillac sent over 1,400 employees to a four-day Edward Deming quality training program at a cost of $650 per employee. IBM-Rochester provides about 45,000 student-days of training a year to its nearly 8,000 employees, and Xerox estimates that it has invested more than $125 million in quality training. But training pays off. Motorola calculates that it earns $30 for every $1 invested in quality training. Training for quality which may focus on developing skills and abilities necessary to perform well as a team member, directly supports collective responsibility.

EVALUATION SYSTEMS

Evaluation systems are crucial because what gets measured is what gets done. Although Deming himself objects to individual performance appraisal, it is still used by most of the winners of the Baldridge Award. These appraisals are consistent with the self-focused U.S. culture. Westinghouse uses a MBO performance review system, with quality improvement as a major criterion for evaluation. Deming opposes MBO because it is driven by outcomes rather than process, and it emphasizes quantitative rather than qualitative results. Yet MBO can be modified to emphasize processes and to set quality rather than quantity goals. Judy Olian, who is the director of the IBM-TQ project at the University of Maryland, suggests that quality goals should be set using two techniques: benchmarking and system goals, rather than individual goals. Her approach helps lessen competition and increase cooperation among employees.

Some of the American companies that have won the Baldridge Award are known for the quality goals they set. For example, Motorola, which has already cut defects from six thousand per million to only forty per million in just five years, has a goal of further cutting defects by 90 percent every two years throughout the 1990s. Quality criteria are often included in employee performance evaluations. Federal Express rates employees on both quality of work and customer service. Xerox evaluates employees on an individual basis, but contribution to the team is one important criterion for evaluation. Performance rating does not have to be competitive. Individuals can compete against absolute standards and not against each other.

REWARD SYSTEMS AND RECOGNITION PROGRAMS

All the companies integrate rewards based on individual and team performance. At Xerox, individuals are nominated for the President's Award or the Xerox Achievement Award. Teams compete for the Excellence Award and the Excellence in Customer Satisfaction Award. Motorola sponsors a Team Quality Olympics where teams make formal presentations of their contributions and receive gold, silver and bronze medals accordingly. Westinghouse has implemented peer review for determining its quality achievement winners.

It is interesting to note that Deming opposes the competitive climate. He argues that cooperation rather than competition is needed. The midpoint between a highly competitive climate and Deming's approach is a system that encourages competition against objective standards of excellence, rather than pitting employees against one another.

In addition to the individually based pay systems, there are also organizationally based pay systems of profit sharing and gain sharing. Though individual incentive pay is prevalent in the most successful Fortune 1,000 companies the reward practices used by over 50 percent of these companies include nonmonetary recognition, team incentives, knowledge/skill-based pay, and cafeteria-style benefits. Additional pay systems that tie monetary rewards to performance at the organizational level include employee stock ownership plans, profit sharing, and gain sharing.

PROMOTION AND CAREER DEVELOPMENT

Few significant changes have been made in the areas of promotion and career development by companies awarded the National Quality Award. The only exception is Federal Express, where new applicants were screened by peers. As for promotion decisions, in order to reduce expensive hierarchies of management, experts in the field recommend deemphasizing the importance of upward promotion and suggest developing new promotion strategies, including job rotation, liaison assignments, opportunities for continuous learning, and entrepreneurial assignments.

HEALTH AND SAFETY

Health issues are of major concern at the organizational level of each of the winning company. Concern for the quality of working life is a characteristic of the philosophy of quality improvement; in that sense, employees can be viewed as the customers of their employing organization.

Although the role of unions has not been examined by Blackburn and Benson, we know that cooperation of the union is crucial for the successful implementation of quality improvement.[8] A positive example is the Saturn Corporation cooperative labor-management relationship. It clearly states that the company and the union are partners and that the role of the union is one of facilitating employees, involvement in the running of the business and in producing high-quality products.

To this point, discussion has highlighted successful U.S. QI programs that include a strong focus on the individual level in terms of evaluation and rewards. However, as the following example shows, it is possible to implement QI effectively with a major focus on the team level, even in a self-focused culture like the United States.

Xerox CEO David Kearns, one of the recipients of the 1989 Baldridge Award, describes how his company implemented quality improvement the American way, including organizational and team components.[9] In the mid-1970s, Xerox found itself out of step with its customers' needs, losing market share to Japanese manufacturers entering the U.S. market with inexpensive desk-top copiers. Xerox discovered that the reject rate of copiers manufactured in the United States was much higher than in Japan. In response, recognizing that quality improvement cannot be measured against internal standards, Xerox began conducting market surveys and interviewing unsatisfied customers. At the same time, visits to the Japanese affiliate, Fuji Xerox, revealed that quality in manufacturing does not increase real cost. It actually decreases cost by reducing rejects, eliminating excessive inspections and field service, and diminishing the cost of business lost to competitors. As a result, Xerox entered the 1980s with a new vision. The manufacturing organization adopted statistical quality control, with an emphasis on preventing defects rather than screening them through inspection.

In addition, Xerox recruited volunteers among its employees to form quality improvement circles. After being trained in interpersonal skills, group dynamics, and problem-solving techniques, employees were asked to evaluate problematic situations and to make recommendations for improvements. This experiment led to training all production workers in partnership with the union.

To support its quality improvement efforts further, Xerox developed cross-organization task teams. In 1983, Xerox introduced leadership through quality a management system that depends heavily on employee involvement and focuses the entire company on the achievement of total quality by giving priority to customer satisfaction. The first step was to train managers in their own groups. The training was usually conducted off-site for about three-and-a-half days. Emphasis was placed on identifying quality shortfalls and the problems that caused them. To assure commitment to the program, training began with the top tier family work group. It then cascaded through the organization, spreading to some 100,000 employees. Xerox changed the role of first-line supervisor from control to that of a coach. In addition, the company set benchmarks for quality from their toughest competitors. For example, they benchmarked L. L. Bean for distribution procedures, Deere Company for central computer operations, Proctor & Gamble for marketing, and Florida Power and Light for its own quality process.

Approximately 240 different functional areas of the company now benchmark against comparable areas in other companies. The employee-involvement teams have been given more authority, including that to stop the line when they identify problems. The key to success has been employee involvement, from top to bottom, including the participation of union leaders. A committed union shares the vision of management and is willing to collaborate when there is a need for change. As a result, Xerox has reported a 45 percent cost reduction and substantial quality improvement in purchased parts from 92 percent defect free to 99.5 percent defect free over the past five years. Production line defective parts have been reduced more than 90 percent since 1982 and the average manufacturing cost reduced by 20 percent.

QI in Britain

The following case demonstrates why the CEO of a large shipyard in Britain failed to implement a quality improvement program successfully. Prior to his appointment as CEO, of the shipyard, John Jones served in the British navy for fifteen years. During this time, he developed an authoritative leadership style. In his first year as CEO, he visited Japan and was impressed with the activity of the quality control circles (QCCs) he saw in a shipyard there. Upon return from his tour he decided to try quality control circles in his shipyard. He called a meeting of all the senior executives, told them about his plan, and instructed them to start the implementation within the next three months. This was Jack's first mistake. Instead of being actively involved with the program and working to instill vision in the upper management team and the workers, he "commanded" that QCCs be created.

In addition, he failed to train himself or his management team in developing and managing quality circles. Not knowing much about the Japanese method, the top executives were reluctant to lead the change. They did not have the understanding of how to do it, why to do it, and what it might mean for them personally. It is no wonder that they could not get their subordinates' understanding and commitment to the program.

The executive team at the British shipyard had also been trained by a different approach to solving quality problems. Employees had not been responsible for solving the problems; they had been mainly the responsibility of the managers and the designated technical experts in quality assurance. For this shipyard to implement quality control circles effectively, the CEO needed to change the traditional approach to quality control. This could have been accomplished through training, restructuring of the organization and of jobs, and a change in organizational culture toward becoming more participative and group focused, to fit both the philosophy and practice of Quality Control Circles. Merely copying what Jack Stone witnessed in Japanese organizations would not work.

In line with this conclusion, Japan Management Association, which is Japan's largest consulting firm and which also operates in Europe, makes a clear distinction between Japanese production techniques (such as integrated production lines and just-in-time) and the motivational methods effective in Japan. The consulting firm sticks strictly to the implementation of the Japanese production techniques. Britain and much of western Europe are self-focused cultures; Japanese motivational techniques will not fit the self-motives of employees in these countries.

We emphasize once again that the key to implementing QI programs in self-focused cultures with a low power differential like Britain is to achieve a balance of team and individual level components. Wright and Brading from the Hay Management Consultants in the United Kingdom propose that good practice in modern British performance management is evolving to provide a balance in the following ways:

- Less focus on retrospective performance assessment and more concentration on future performance planning and improvement

- Identification and recognition of skills and competencies associated with higher levels of performance

- Identification and recognition of outputs that are defined in qualitative terms, not just quantitative ones

- A free, upwardly managed process

- A more coaching and counseling style of appraisal and less focus on criticism

- More focus on the individual contribution to success of the team as a whole, with some objectives defined in these terms

- An equal concern with improving performance as with assessing it

- No forced distribution of ratings (so no win-lose scenarios)

- No formal rating given, as a possibility
- An integrated pay system which reinforces the following aspects of performance:
  - The potential contribution of individuals to the team in terms of their technical skills and competencies
  - The actual contribution of individuals to the team in terms of the successful application of those skills and competence
  - The actual output of the individual
  - The success achieved by the team
  - The success achieved by the organization

Those aspects of performance can be linked to three types of remuneration: base pay structure, differential pay awards, and bonuses. Base pay should be tied to both the potential and the actual contribution of employees. Differential pay awards should be linked to actual contribution and actual output of individual employees. Bonuses should depend on actual contribution, actual output of individual employees, success achieved by teams, and success achieved by the organization.

Similar to the U.S culture, QI programs in Britain should be set up to evaluate and reward employees on both the team and individual levels. Given that Britain is a self-focused culture, personal accountability is important to employees. Further, managers should focus on acting as coaches with a goal of improving performance. This approach, which is more likely to empower employees is appropriate to Britain's low power distance. Finally, there should be a strong focus on continuous improvement as well as encouraging cooperation by rewarding team activities and adjusting performance reviews. Although both are classified as self-focused and low-power-differential nations, Britain is more collectivistic in nature and values cooperation more highly than the United States. Avoiding strategies that foster competition among workers (for example, forced distribution of ratings) distinguishes the British system of quality improvement from the American one.

QI in Developing Countries

The growing trend toward globalization of business has affected developing countries in at least two ways. First, many multinational firms in industrialized countries (United States, Germany, and Japan, for instance) have set up manufacturing plants in developing countries in South America and east Asia. A major motivation for this trend is the low cost of labor in those countries. Second, these nations often wish to enter the world market through increasing their own exports.

Whether we look at multinationals setting up plants in these countries or domestic firms attempting to produce goods for export, a central issue is quality. In the case of multinationals, the competitive advantage gained from lower labor cost may be lost if it is not accompanied by a high level of product quality. For domestic firms in these countries to attract buyers for their goods, they must prove their quality. In fact, many firms find that to compete globally they must acquire ISO-9000 certification(which qualifies products for exportation).[10]

Thus many manufacturing plants in developing countries have been attempting a dramatic change from very poor to very high product quality. For example, in one of the *maquiladora* (foreign-owned multinationals operating in Mexico) plants producing flexible printed circuits, the defect rate in 1990 was 25 percent, on-time delivery was not achieved in 35 percent to 40 percent of the cases, and employee turnover was 20 percent. Now those numbers have improved dramatically: defects have been reduced to a few per-million, on-time delivery has climbed up to 96 percent, and turnover is running at only 9 percent. The overall improvement in productivity between 1990 and 1992 was 67 percent.[11] Similarly the auto industry in Argentina, Brazil, and Mexico has been going through significant improvements in quality and competitiveness. Both Brazil and Argentina have an integrated motor industry, making everything from engine blocks to radios; by 1996, Fiat will buy 69 percent of its components from suppliers in Brazil.[12] The prospect for the South American car industry is viewed so positively that some people even say that "if you are lucky, your next car will be made in Mexico."[13]

Yet many multinational companies still have difficulties in running their manufacturing plants in Latin America. Four of the major problems that can be cited are the lack of technical knowledge and training, the lack of strong work values (which results in a high level of turnover) the lack of advanced technology, and the instability of the governments.

The first two problems represent the human side of quality improvement. Managers and workers will be motivated to change their work values and to acquire knowledge and skills if they know how these changes will benefit them. Therefore an effective program of QI in developing countries should take into consideration the cultural characteristics that shape workers' self-concept and self-identity, and should develop a program that responds to those values.

The dominant cultural values of most developing countries are high group focus and high power differential. In Mexico, for example, there is a strong emphasis on the family. People work to make a living, not to develop a career, because career life competes with the family. Therefore, if a relative gets sick or needs some kind of assistance, a worker will quit in order to help out. That situation helps explain the high rate of absenteeism and turnover.[14]

The high respect for authority and emphasis on family and group belongingness should be taken into consideration when implementing QI programs in developing countries. Our 3-D model of QI serves as a general guideline for developing the specific programs. Starting on the organizational level, QI programs should be initiated and continuously supported by top-level management. Top level executives should begin the implementation of ISO-9000. They should clarify to the employees that both the companies' survival, and the economy of the country at large depend on getting the accreditation of ISO-9000. Top-level managers actively should serve as quality auditors and should direct the QI programs. Managing by facts is an imperative; therefore efforts should be exerted to develop information systems that will allow data collection on performance measures, continuous monitoring, and the provision of feedback on quality improvement. Top-down communication should be enhanced by having high level management teams exchange information and ideas with their workers, both in writing and orally.

The issue of communication requires a word of caution to mutinational firms attempting to do business in developing nations—or for that matter in any country whose national language is different from their own. In order to have top managers actively involved in the communication process, they must *be able* to communicate. This necessity points toward selecting middle and upper management with the skills to communicate in the language workers understand. If expatriates are used in management positions, they should be trained and encouraged to learn the language. It may prove best to develop managers from the country where the company is located. These managers will have the advantage of speaking the language, knowing the culture, and acting as role models that the lower-level workers may respond to more positively. At a minimum, we suggest that at least the HRM manager be fluent in the language and culture of that country; the HR department may conduct the most communication and coordination with workers.

The design of training programs is crucial to the success of QI. Unskilled employees in developing countries must learn to tell a good part from a bad one and to interpret specifications laid down by sophisticated customers. Training programs should be designed for team leaders, teams, and individuals. On the team level, training should focus on three major parts: technical knowledge and skills, statistical knowledge for dealing with data, and the interpersonal skills necessary for effective groups. On the individual level, training programs that lead workers to become self-inspectors or quality auditors are highly effective.

Training programs in developing countries may also need to focus on fundamental skills like reading, writing, and basic mathematics. One must remember that illiteracy rates in these countries is often quite high. If businesses expect technical and statistical training to be useful, they must see to it that workers have the basic skill level to understand it. Since it may be difficult to hire workers who already possess sufficient educational background, businesses may be required to supply that basic training themselves.

The human resource management practices in developing countries should correspond to cultural values. For example, a sense of group belongingness is fostered by forming functional teams that also function as QI teams. The most effective rewards in a group-focused culture are based on teams and on the organization. In addition, benefits that include medical, health care and retirement programs are highly appreciated. At the same time, merit pay increases are not part of the typical culture in developing countries. They decrease group cohesiveness and violate the norm of being part of the group. Furthermore piecework incentive systems may backfire if used in these group-focused, family-oriented cultures. In Mexico, one *maquiladora* tried to develop weekly quotas, with the understanding that workers would be paid incentives for production numbers reached over quota. After the quotas were reached, the workers quit for the week to spend time with their families. Yet this same cultural value of family suggests a method to reduce turnover rates. With the practice of "word of mouth" hiring in Mexico, family members are often the first ones to be engaged. Family ties may then help to overcome the problem.

The most successful QI programs in developing countries should be ones that are initiated, monitored, and directed by top-level management; ones that are based on teams, emphasize training of teams and individuals, and adjust the HRM practices to the dominant cultural values. The requirement to meet the standards of ISO-9000 makes QI programs in developing countries an imperative.

Table 8.1

*Implementation of Quality Improvement Programs in Countries with Low
and High Group Focus and Low and High Power Differentials*

	Low Power Differential	High Power Differential
Self-focused		
Cultural profile	*Entrepreneur*	*Oldest Child*
Interventions		
Organization wide	Empowerment	Centralized control
Team level	Second to personal quality	Second to personal quality
Individual level	Individual training	Individual training
	Individual responsibility	Individual responsibility
	Individual feedback	Individual feedback
	Individual problem solving	Individual problem solving
	Individual performance evaluation	Individual performance evaluation
	Individual rewards	Individual rewards
Examples	United States, Australia, Britain, New Zealand	South Africa, France, Italy, Spain
Group-focused		
Cultural profile	*Collective Rebel*	*Model Citizen*
Interventions		
Organization wide	Self-management	Team leadership
Team level	Team training	Team training
	Team responsibility	Team responsibility
	Team feedback	Team feedback
	Team problem solving	Team problem solving
	Team performance evaluation	Team performance evaluation
	Team rewards	Team rewards
Individual level	Second to teams	Second to teams
Examples	Israel, Costa Rica, Norway	Japan, Korea, Singapore, Brazil

Summary

Quality improvement is effective in every culture when managers
have a clear vision of its purpose for the organization, both for
themselves and for their employees. QI programs must be tailored
toward the values of a particular culture. Moreover, the programs
must be developed so as to foster the perception of employees that

their participation will help fulfill their self-motives for enhancement and growth. Additionally both a self-focus and a group-focus seem to be important for the successful implementation of QI in self-focused cultures. QI programs in organizations need to be supported by policies and strategies that allow people to be active participants and that reward them for their improvement.

The 3-D model of quality improvement serves as a prototype for implementing quality improvement programs across cultures and organizational settings, from manufacturing to services. QI programs are more likely to succeed if they are implemented at the appropriate organizational level of analysis (top-management, team, or individual level), as specified in Table 8.1 given the cultural norms of the country or area.

9

The Complete
Global Manager

Although tradition and inertia inhibit the development of fresh perspectives on how people think and act, we have attempted to overcome this inertia by rethinking what "being ourselves" really means to an employee. We have done so because the globalization of companies has shown us that managerial practices and motivational techniques common in one country often work poorly in another. Thus the differences between nations and cultures has become as important for understanding work actions as the differences between individuals. What is the final stage? *Watching managers implement these ideas to successfully manage in their companies*. We now return to the lessons provided in this book, followed by an action plan for using it to become a more effective manager.

The First Lesson: How to Use Self-Knowledge
to Be a More Effective Manager

The first and perhaps most important lesson from our book concerns a manager's assessment of self knowledge and cultural values as well as those of the manager's subordinates. If you have not already done so, we strongly recommend that you use the assessment tool that we provide in the Appendix in order to assess your self-knowledge. What do these scales provide? They give you a basic understanding of how you think about the world and your work environment. Once equipped with this information, you can understand why you might have a general tendency to use certain management styles over others. For instance, maybe you think about the world in self-focused terms, and you have a very high growth motive. What does this mean for your management style? You are likely to prefer a "take charge" style of managing employees, and you will give people very challenging work assignments so that the "cream" will rise to the top. What about a very high self-consistency motive? One very successful manager from Eli Lilly Pharmaceuticals reminds us of this motive. This regional sales manager has been extremely successful at Lilly, and corporate headquarters has approached him a number of times to come "in-house" (return to corporate headquarters in Indianapolis), so that he can continue climbing the Lilly hierarchy. However, he really enjoys his current home and surroundings and knows that he does his job very well. He has commented that he is very pleased with his job, career focus, and life-style and says, "Why should I give this all up, just to compete with those hungry guys in Indianapolis?" His high motive for consistency makes him value his current position and status.

So what steps can you as managers take now that you have mastered our approach to self-knowledge and understanding? There are seven basic steps to follow.

1. *Assess your self-motives and cultural values.* See how you compare with other managers using the comparison information provided in the Appendix.

2. *Ask your subordinates to fill out the assessment tool.* We suggest that you tell them that you are trying to develop a better sense of the ideas and issues that they value. Also it is important to let them score the tool themselves since it helps create commitment to its results.

3. *Share the results with one another in a group discussion session.* such a session helps everyone understand each other's viewpoints, and you will get insights into how others think.

4. *Assess the management style that you are currently using with your subordinates.* As a beginning, we suggest that you focus on those topics that you have read about in the book and that are of interest to you right away. Once you have a firm understanding of the self-knowledge approach, you will have no problem extending your diagnoses to other management areas, such as negotiation, performance appraisals, and the like.

5. *Ask yourself whether or not your self-knowledge and values match those of your subordinates and the management style that you are currently using.* Is there a good match? If not, where does the mismatch seem to lie? Remember, it is much easier to change your managerial style than it is to change people's cultural values.

6ᴀ. *Assume for a moment that there is a good match between your values, those of your subordinates, and the managerial style used in your workplace.* Ask yourself how to fine-tune the situation or what additional things you can do to complement the self-motives of your subordinates.

6ʙ. *Assume for a moment that there is a mismatch between your values, those of your subordinates, and the managerial style used.* What is the source of this mismatch? Can you adjust your managerial style so that it is more aligned with your employees? Perhaps you are using a style that is contrary to your nature. Often we find that such a mismatch creates unnecessary tension for everyone.

7. *Create a new work environment.* If there is a mismatch or a weak match between self-knowledge and managerial style, it is time to create a new work context. How can you do this? One way is to make people aware of their values so that they can understand why their basic reaction to certain styles is so strong at times. For instance, a group-focused manager who is asked to "divide and conquer" some existing work groups may feel intensely uncomfortable at setting up competitions among employees. Many times, this discomfort reflects the fact that the manager is just unaware of the mismatch ("I don't like it, but I'm not quite sure why"). You'll be surprised at how powerful awareness of self-knowledge can be in improving the workplace. Much of the time, people are at odds with one another simply because they don't understand each other's intent. Another procedure to follow is to share with your subordinates how you want them to work (e.g., types of projects) and how it fits in with their personal motives.

By following these seven basic steps, managers can greatly improve work surroundings and the way their work groups perform with one another. This approach helps new group members understand the underlying values of the work group as well, and it can be used as an aid for socialization.

We have provided an additional guide that you can use in trying to understand what the likely motives and values of other managers may be if you cannot directly assess this information. In Table 2.1, we listed a number of examples that represent a range of self-focused to group-focused cultures and low-power-differential to high-power-differential countries. We emphasize, however, that this categorization scheme illustrates the typical person from a listed country; not everyone in every culture is the same. For instance, a particular French manager might be more self-focused than a Canadian manager, depending on each person's unique experiences. Therefore we strongly encourage you to complete the self-assessment tool as well.

The Second Lesson: How We Can Understand Ourselves and Others

What has been learned from our approach to people and culture? We have presented some very basic ideas with some very powerful implications. With our approach, we have focused on linking various levels in an organization, including culture, management practices, and employee action and thinking (attitudes toward work, job satisfaction, and productivity). The way that people think about the world can only be discovered by looking at how people view themselves—their self-knowledge. But this is only part of the picture. Culture and national values serve as a general guide to (and management practices as a more immediate influence on) work activities. Using a human perspective, we have developed a way to link a person's culture, management practices, and employee activities through our self-knowledge approach. We can summarize the ideas as follows:

- Effective managers must understand their own self-knowledge as well as that of their employees.
- Effective managers need to appreciate and acknowledge the differences that people have in their general, cultural values.
- Effective managers must understand their own work environment.

Our approach of cultural self-knowledge consists of four core pieces:

1. Self-knowledge, which is shaped by culture and personal experiences and consists of three primary motives—

enhancement (wanting to feel good about oneself), growth (wanting to develop and challenge oneself), and consistency (wanting continuity and stability in life).

2. Culture, which is the shared way that a group of people think about the world.

3. Management practices, which simply refers to the way that people manage their employees on the job

4. Work Action, which results from people's self knowledge and culture.

Self-knowledge helps us judge and understand managerial practices that, in turn direct employee action. If a management practice (for example, TQM) is judged positively by an employee, it is more likely to improve that individual's productivity because he or she will be committed to the practice than if it been judged negatively. Cultural values also play an important role in implementing management practices since they serve as another way to judge those practices.

How are management practices assessed as effective or ineffective? They are successful if they contribute to a personal and a group sense of self-worth. Cultural values like a self-versus a group focus determine people's views of the relative merits of various managerial practices and influence their reactions to these practices. In Sweden, management that emphasizes worker participation, equality, and worker control is praised by employees and managers alike. At Hyundai of South Korea, management focuses on a paternalistic style of leadership consistent with the Korean emphasis on Confucianism.

Understanding Self-Knowledge

As just stated there are three basic motives that people need to understand in order to have complete self-knowledge. First, everyone wants to feel good about themselves in their day-to-day lives. Much of what people do derives from their desire to feel appreciated and to believe that their life has worth and merit. Managers who use some basic principles of praise and recognition often find astounding success in motivating their employees. Take, for example, the actions of Japanese or Korean managers as they work to maintain "face." In one sense, the Asian concept of face is similar (although not identical) to the notion of self-enhancement. In the case of group-focused countries, the desire to feel good extends from people to their valued friends and work colleagues.

Second, people like to challenge themselves, and to learn new things about their world. People's desire for growth is seen in many ways —a manager who works weekends in order to learn a new computer system or a secretary who takes night classes in accounting to move into a new bookkeeping position. People set new goals for themselves, and they work hard to achieve them.

Third, people want some continuity and stability in their lives. An important question that people ask themselves when confronted with a new situation is, "Is this really me?" As people face their work environment, they ask themselves whether or not they are comfortable doing various tasks, working with new people, and thinking new ideas. Although individuals certainly enjoy learning about new ideas, as the growth motive suggests, they often ask themselves whether or not something is really true to their basic nature. People even ask this question as they confront new fashions in dress, philosophy, and life-style.

Understanding Culture

The desire to understand how people's cultural values influences managerial practices and employee activities is what led us to develop our model. One way to think about culture and management is by using the metaphor of an automobile that needs to be diagnosed and fixed. According to this thinking, an effective manager is a good mechanic who really knows how to understand a problem before fixing it (or trading in the car for a new one). What underlies this metaphor is a potential difference in cultural values—namely, the "I can fix it" approach versus the "I have to understand it on its own terms" one. Although both approaches can be used to manage in a company successfully (just as different types of word processors can produce the same annual report), they reflect very basic differences in values and thinking.

A very important way of viewing people's cultural values is by looking at their self- versus group focus. We have used this way of thinking as an important part of understanding how employees' self-motives will be satisfied. For instance, employees from a self-focused culture will look to their personal accomplishments and work progress as a way of assessing self-growth, whereas people from a group-focused culture will look to the accomplishments of valued work colleagues. Thus the American employee asks the question, "How can I do this job better?" while the Korean employee asks, "How can we coordinate our efforts to improve our group's performance?"

Another important part of a person's cultural values is what we call the power differential, or a feeling that people are equal or unequal in their power. People from high-power-differential countries such as Mexico or Singapore believe that superiors have a basic right to give commands to their subordinates and that these should not second-guess or question their superiors. It is not that managers impose an authoritarian style against our other employees' wishes; rather, this style is what is expected. Thus the participative management styles that companies may wish their managers to use may be at odds with employees' general values. For instance, Mary Teagarden talks about the experience of an American manager sent to Mexico to run a *maquiladora* plant.[1] As part of his desire to make friends and show his immediate subordinates an open relationship, he invited them to visit his home across the border in Arizona. After several unsuccessful tries at getting them to visit for dinner, the manager began to think that his subordinates were snubbing him. In reality, he had made the mistake of trying to lower the power differences between himself and his subordinates. Not only did they resist this attempt but they resented the idea that he tried to break down the power differential. Why? In a high-power-differential country like Mexico, a person's status is reaffirmed by how superiors (powerful people) treat the person. The American manager unintentionally sent the message, "You aren't worthy of me treating you formally!"

Understanding Management Practices

There are a number of important lessons that managers can learn about many of the practices that they use. For instance, managers can increase employees' understanding of one another through effective communication. Effective communication means that people from different cultures share an understanding of the words and ideas. These rules are the product of people's cultural backgrounds and personal experiences. Shared understanding can be gained by learning more about others' cultures.

Another example comes from our discussion of developing teamwork. In some countries like the United States, Australia, and Britain, the basic idea of a team is a group of people who don't get in one another's way too much and who help each other get things that they personally desire. In other countries like Sweden, Japan, and Israel, a team is an accepted and fundamental way that people think about others around them. Their team means those people to whom an individual has an intense loyalty and attachment. How do managers build this kind of team? The question itself is suspect since team membership is a lifelong obligation and not something that can be manipulated or easily constructed. Taken to this extreme, the team is something best created by relying on people's natural friendships outside of work.

Understanding Work Behavior

In the end, the purpose of our approach has been to help managers understand what work practices can be used, changed, or adapted to increase their personal productivity as well as that of their subordinates. Perhaps the most important point to make here is that these work outcomes are not simply job performance. Yes, managers want their employees to be more productive. However, there are other important results to consider, such as job satisfaction and turnover. Managers may have very productive employees who quit and go to another company because they can get their self-motives fulfilled elsewhere—and the productive employee is the one who can most easily change companies. As managers work in the global environment, they must remember that there are a variety of rewards that they can use to be effective managers.

The Third Lesson: Management Practices Using Self-Knowledge

In order to put our principles into practice, we now turn back to Table 8.2, which illustrates a number of different managerial styles and techniques that are effective in various countries. For the remainder of this chapter, we will examine a number of techniques for each of the four basic types of cultures (refer to Chapter 3 for a refresher of these four types): *entrepreneur* (self-focus and low power differential), *oldest child* (self-focus and high power differential), *collective rebel* (group focus and low power differential), and *model citizen* (group focus and high power differential). As we will remind the reader, a person's self-motives may vary within any culture grouping, and a given managerial technique may have to be reoriented for that person. For instance, in Chapter 3, we discussed two fictitious British employees, Alfred and Nigel. Even though they both of them came from the same culture (entrepreneur), their self-motives were quite different, and they respond individually to the same management techniques. Alfred, who is high on the enhancement and growth scales, responds well to individual recognition and job challenges. Nigel, who is high on enhancement but low on growth, responds well to individual recognition but does not want a lot of new job challenges. They share a self-focus (they look to their personal accomplishments). What they don't share is a desire for new job challenges. As you read through the next section, keep in mind these types of differences in self-motives. Also, as we've emphasized earlier, you should keep in mind that not everyone from a single country has the same cultural values even though most people do. This fact is why we recommend that you use our diagnostic tool in the Appendix for your specific work situation.

Entrepreneur

In this cultural group found, for example, in the United States, England, and Australia, there is a self-focus and a low power differential. People think about themselves as unique individuals, and there is a strong emphasis on equality. Each person has an equal say, and managers are not expected to place excessive demands on their subordinates.

What are some of the managerial techniques one might use for the entrepreneurial culture? One obvious choice would be goal setting or MBO.[2] According to goal setting, people who have specific and challenging goals are more productive and motivated than those who have more general or vague objectives. This motivational technique has been shown effective for logging crews, tire workers, computer programmers, and college professors, among others. The technique is very appropriate for an entrepreneurial culture because it focuses on furnishing each employee with his or her individualized work objectives and it provides for personal initiative in selecting these. Goal setting might not be as useful, of course, if an employee has a low motive for growth.

Another motivational approach that we discussed is that of job enrichment—improving motivation by adding variety, responsibility, importance, and so forth. This approach increases the variety of skills needed on the job, makes clear to employees the importance of their work, increases the sense of personal attachment to a task, and provides employees with both personal autonomy and responsibility and individual performance appraisals. For this technique to be effective in an entrepreneurial culture, many of these innovations need to be initiated by the employees themselves. If a person has a high consistency motive, there will be a problem with the type of disruption and change brought on by an extensive job enrichment program.

Communication in an entrepreneurial culture needs to rely on individual initiative, and it will flow freely in an organization. It is not uncommon for employees to cross organizational boundaries and initiate discussions with superiors who are several organizational levels above themselves. In addition, employees freely discuss their own ideas with their colleagues. A prime example of this communication style is the open-door policy and open-office environment, found in many U.S. companies such as Hewlett Packard and John Deere.

Teams have become increasingly popular in the United States. In such an entrepreneurial culture, teams must be put together recognizing individual diversity and accomplishments. Group activities must never stand in the way of a person's autonomy and liberty. Therefore techniques such as participation must be based on individual actions rather than collective behavior.

Finally, leadership in an entrepreneurial culture focuses on establishing a unique relationship between the leader and follower. This relationship is direct and personal; the leader is not a remote power figure or a person who relates to a follower as if he or she is one of many. Effective leaders provide their followers with the encouragement and skills to help them help themselves.

Oldest Child

In this cultural group found, for example, in France, Germany, and Italy, there is a self-focus and a high power differential. People think about themselves as singular individuals, and there is a strong emphasis on the chain-of-command. Each person has a unique but unequal say, and managers are not expected to place excessive demands on their subordinates.

What are some of the managerial techniques one might use for the oldest-child culture? As with the entrepreneurial culture, goal setting would be effective. This technique is very appropriate because it focuses on providing each employee with his or her individualized work objectives. However, unlike the entrepreneurial case of relying on individual initiative, in an oldest-child culture employees seek goals assigned from their superiors and rely on directives from "above." There is an assumed legitimacy of superiors assigning work objectives to their subordinates.

Similarly, job enrichment may be quite successful although the focus on individual initiative needs to be less emphasized. The key here is to provide employees with an opportunity to have variety and challenge in their jobs but provided through proper channels. In other words, a German worker will respond positively to individually tailored job challenges provided they are instituted using the existing company hierarchy and labor structure. In fact, the apprenticeship system used nationwide in Germany is renown for its emphasis on challenging, multiyear training (usually three years). This system is recognized as a legitimate part of labor, and it is a system that is highly enriched by U.S. standards. Not only do apprentices learn about many jobs and tasks within their area of expertise but they learn also about the principles underlying their jobs (for instance an electrician learns about wiring and the physics that goes with it). The system of apprenticeship is legitimate in the eyes of employees because it is implemented nationally.

Communication in an oldest-child culture needs to rely on both individual initiative and the existing chains-of-command. The organizational systems found in countries such as France and Germany are quite bureaucratic. This situation is reflected in communication, which occurs through "proper channels." It is uncommon for employees to cross organizational boundaries and initiate discussions with superiors who are several organizational levels above themselves. However, employees freely discuss their own ideas with their colleagues. So while executives from Daimler-Benz and Siemens-Nixdorf communicate directly with shop-floor workers, such exchanges occur through the system of codetermination that we described earlier in our book.

Finally, leadership in an oldest-child culture focuses on establishing a unique relationship between leader and follower. This relationship is characterized by a one-on-one connection between leader and follower, and by an emphasis on the leader as a powerful figure in the follower's life. In terms of national histories, we see that France, Italy, and Germany have had a number of powerful (sometimes infamous) leaders. Leaders are larger than life but treat their followers as distinctive and valuable. Effective leaders provide their followers with the encouragement and skills to help them help themselves. A nice example of this type of leader is Luciano Benetton, one of the family responsible for the Italian company bearing that name. He and his sister, Giuliana, cofounded Benetton in 1965 as a subsidiary of the IVEP Group. Luciano who has long been viewed as a leader to whom employees from all organizational levels are loyal, also focuses on each retail storeowner as a unique contributor to the Benetton enterprise.

Collective Rebel

In this cultural group found, for example in Sweden, and Israel, there is a group-focus and a low power differential. People think about themselves as equal to one another, and there is a strong emphasis on group memberships. Each person has the same amount of say, managers are not expected to place excessive demands on their subordinates, and group memberships (work groups, family groups, and so forth) are very important .

What are some of the managerial techniques one might use for the collective-rebel culture? Participation, which often takes place in a group setting and is therefore, endorsed by group-focused cultures, would be one. Participation is also appropriate for a low power and status differential culture. Participation contributes to employees' sense of self-worth; it includes everyone in decision making, and provides opportunities for group belonging-ness. If a manager wants to use a motivational technique such as goal setting, then goals should be set participatively and should be established for the work group and not just each individual.

Earlier we discussed job enrichment. For this technique to work in a collective-rebel culture, many of its innovations need to be initiated by the employees themselves *as team members*. For instance we have referred to the Swedish system of combining the social environment with the demands of technology. Volvo redesigned its assembly-line operation so that work groups were kept intact and allowed to have control over the production process as a group.[3] Job rotation among group members, group autonomy and responsibility, group performance appraisals, and the like are part of the autonomous work groups used in Sweden and Norway. Both methods increase employee motivation and a sense of self-worth arising from the success of the work group.

Communication in a collective-rebel culture needs to rely on the group, and it will flow freely in an organization. It is not uncommon for employees to cross organizational boundaries and initiate discussions with superiors who are several organizational levels above themselves. In addition, employees freely discuss their own ideas with their colleagues. However, conversations and discussion are likely to take place within rather than across work groups. Relying on cross-functional teams may be more difficult than it would be in an entrepreneurial culture.

Finally, leadership in a collective-rebel culture focuses on relating to the group rather than, establishing a unique relationship with a follower. In this culture, a leader is readily approachable by followers, is not very different from them, and identifies with the needs of important groups.

Model Citizen

In this cultural group found, for example, in Brazil, Mexico, and South Korea, there is a group-focus and a high power differential. People think about themselves in terms of their group member-ships, and there is a strong emphasis on hierarchy and status. Each person has a place on a ladder; managers may place high demands on their subordinates.

What are some of the managerial techniques one might use for the model-citizen culture? One obvious choice is the quality cir-cle, such as that used in Japan. In Japanese quality circles, people work in teams in order to provide job innovations, suggestions, and analysis of work settings. QCs often take a substantial amount of time away from employees' time and require a great deal of effort and persistence. Many of these QCs are created by company execu-tives who are also joined together in large, nationally sponsored col-lections of QCs. In other words, the QCs are often a management tool that is imposed on groups of employees. In the model-citizen culture, techniques such as participation must be based on individ-ual contributions to groups, and these are directed by a superior in a hierarchy. For example, Daihatsu employees in South Korea are very team oriented but have a strong allegiance to their company's executives and CEO.

Communication in a good-citizen culture relies on the natu-rally existing connections among group members, and information flows freely within these existing groups. At the same time, the flow between different groups can be quite slow and stunted. Informa-tion sharing is particularly difficult among companies unless they are organized in some larger network, such as the Japanese keiretsu. Employees freely discuss their own ideas with their col-leagues. For instance, SONY executives meet with their managers on a regular basis in order to find out the latest news from the shop floor. These meetings are characterized by a frank discussion of what resources are needed, who is not working up to potential, and what is expected of each team member according to the company's philosophy of strong company commitment. A key variable to con-sider in managing in a model-citizen culture is exactly how big and extensive a "team" can be in an organization. In some good-citizen cultures (for example, Japan), in-groups can extend to entire busi-ness conglomerates. In others (for example, Mexico), in-groups are more closely tied to immediate work colleagues and family.

The *groupware method*, described in Chapter 5, is an example of an adjustment of a group-decision approach to a self-focused culture. Team members communicate through keyboards and a computer screen, and they benefit from group discussion without getting involved in a face-to-face communication. This approach may not be effective in a group-focused culture or in a high power differential culture because it does not provide opportunities for person-to-person interaction, and it breaks down existing authority (e.g., everyone becomes equal in his or her ability to get and send messages) in the organization.

Finally, leadership in a good-citizen culture focuses on a strong, distant leader who is quite powerful and wise. In a country such as Singapore, the leaders of companies provide employees with firm rules concerning how to behave and act, as well as how to lead a correct life. In the good-citizen culture, effective leaders provide their followers with the encouragement and skills to help them; the leader's role is one of the benevolent father figure as in South Korea.

Summary

If we return to Chapter 1, and our initial discussion of culture, what have we really learned? Managers and their employees who work abroad, or even in a different part of their country than the one they are used to, must develop an awareness of cultural differences in managerial practices and principles of behavior. Furthermore, they need to understand why culture makes a difference. This knowledge will enable them more effectively to manage employee actions in response to managerial practices that they might try to implement. We also need consider cultural characteristics when we think about transferring our managerial practices and motivational practices across international boundaries. Management practices must be congruent with cultural and personal values in order to be embraced, and to have a positive impact in the workplace. When these methods do not conform to people's values, they need to be modified to relate to the unique characteristics of targeted employees. Becoming a successful manager abroad, or a successful manager of diverse employees at home, requires a knowledge and understanding of people, their cultural backgrounds, and their unique needs.

APPENDIX

Assessing
Your Cultural Values

The purpose of this short questionnaire is to help you better understand your *self- versus group focus* as well as your *power differential*. Your responses to these questions reflect your general values that are influenced by your culture and your unique experiences. The following questions reflect opinions that you may or may not hold. *Think about your own feelings concerning each of these statements and answer for yourself, not how you think other people would answer.* For each question, place a number in the blank at the right.

1 = I strongly disagree with this statement.
2 = I slightly disagree with this statement.
3 = I neither disagree or agree with this statement.
4 = I slightly agree with this statement.
5 = I strongly agree with this statement.

Self Versus Group-Focus

1. Employees like to work in a group rather than by themselves.   _____

2. It is important for employees to make friends at their jobs.

3. Working as part of a team motivates employees.   _____

4. Problem solving by groups gives better results than problem solving by individuals.   _____

5. Cooperation among team members usually helps to solve problems.   _____

6. Team-based work provides the best work performance.   _____

7. Being part of a team has *no* important benefit for work.   _____

8. Teamwork is central to an effective company.   _____

9. Friendships in an organization are an important part of life.   _____

10. Employees do not like to be put in teams.   _____

Scoring Procedure

Give yourself the number of points on each question that you wrote down. Some of these items were negatively worded so that you need to rescore their value by "reversing" them (if you scored "1," give yourself "5"; if you scored "2," give yourself "4"; if you scored "4," give yourself "2"; and if you scored "5," give yourself "1"). The following items should be scored in reverse: questions 7 and 10. Once you have reversed the scores for these items, add up all ten questions for your grand total.

Total score   _____

1 = I strongly disagree with this statement.
2 = I slightly disagree with this statement.
3 = I neither disagree or agree with this statement.
4 = I slightly agree with this statement.
5 = I strongly agree with this statement.

Power Differential

1. In most situations managers should make decisions without consulting their subordinates. _____

2. In work-related matters, managers have a right to expect obedience from their subordinates. _____

3. Employees who often question authority sometimes keep their managers from being effective. _____

4. Once a top-level executive makes a decision, people working for the company should not question it. _____

5. Employees should not express disagreements with their managers. _____

6. Managers should be able to make the right decisions without consulting with others. _____

7. Managers who let their employees participate in decisions lose power. _____

8. A company's rules should not be broken, not even when the employee thinks it is in the company's best interest. _____

Scoring Procedure

Give yourself the number of points on each question that you wrote down. Add up all eight questions for your grand total.

Total score _____

Assessing
Your Self-Knowledge

The purpose of this short questionnaire is to help you better understand your self-knowledge, including your self-enhancement, self-growth, and self-consistency motives. Your responses to these questions reflect your opinions based on your various life experiences. The following questions solicit opinions that you may or may not hold. *Think about your own feelings concerning each of these statements, and answer for yourself, <u>not</u> how you think other people would answer.* For each question, place a number in the blank at the right.

1 = *I strongly disagree with this statement.*
2 = *I slightly disagree with this statement.*
3 = *I neither disagree or agree with this statement.*
4 = *I slightly agree with this statement.*
5 = *I strongly agree with this statement.*

Self-Enhancement Motive

1. It is important that my own work is recognized. _____

2. I feel proud when the accomplishments of my friends are acknowledged by my company. _____

3. What matters to me at work is feeling good about myself, not necessarily what I am getting paid. _____

4. I am happy when the people who are important to me are satisfied. _____

5. If I am confronted with feedback that I have not been doing as well as I should on one task, I prefer to concentrate on other tasks for which I am doing well. _____

6. I enjoy getting credit from being a member of a successful group. _____

7. It is important to me that others recognize my accomplishments. _____

8. If the people I work with don't feel good about themselves, I just can't work well. _____

9. I feel good about myself when I do things other than my job. _____

10. I feel good when the people I work with help me out of their own free will. _____

Scoring Procedure

Give yourself the number of points on each question that you wrote down. Add up items 1, 3, 5, 7, and 9 to get your score on self-focused enhancement.

Total self-focused enhancement _____

Add up items 2, 4, 6, 8, and 10 to get your score on group-focused enhancement.

Total group-focused enhancement _____

1 = I strongly disagree with this statement.
2 = I slightly disagree with this statement.
3 = I neither disagree or agree with this statement.
4 = I slightly agree with this statement.
5 = I strongly agree with this statement.

Self-Growth Motive

1. It gives me pleasure to learn new skills and challenge myself even it if requires great effort. _____

2. In general, I will usually take on even seemingly impossible challenges. _____

3. I feel a strong sense of personal competence in my work. _____

4. Based on my past work with teams or groups, I feel confident that groups can take on most challenges. _____

5. If my work team has capable people in it, I feel capable. _____

6. A work team can cope with difficult goals with less stress than an individual employee. _____

7. No matter how difficult the job is, I can tackle it. _____

8. I think that it is important for me constantly to learn new ideas and to challenge myself. _____

9. A work group can do its work better by learning new ways to be efficient. _____

10. When I work in a team, I feel more confident that we can get things done. _____

Scoring Procedure

Give yourself the number of points on each question that you wrote down. Add up items 1, 2, 3, 7, and 8 to get your score on self-focused efficacy.

Total self-focused efficacy _____

Add up items 4, 5, 6, 9, and 10 to get your score on group-focused efficacy.

Total group-focused efficacy _____

Add up all ten questions for your grand total _____

1 = I strongly disagree with this statement.
2 = I slightly disagree with this statement.
3 = I neither disagree or agree with this statement.
4 = I slightly agree with this statement.
5 = I strongly agree with this statement.

Self-Consistency Motive

1. I prefer it when I can use standard and familiar procedures for my work. _____

2. It fits me best to work in a company where the top management does not initiate too frequent changes. _____

3. I am most comfortable if the people around me follow accepted work procedures and do not try new approaches. _____

4. I feel uncomfortable if my job makes me act in a way that I am not used to acting. _____

5. It can be disruptive if there are no clear and systematic procedures for promoting people in my company. _____

6. It bothers me when there is a high rate of turnover in my company. _____

7. It is important for me to have a fixed and organized schedule of my work day. _____

8. I like it if my coworkers stay the same just so I work with familiar people day-to-day. _____

9. I have a resistance to changes in work. _____

10. I find it stressful if my job requires me to do things that are out of my character. _____

Scoring Procedure

Give yourself the number of points on each question that you wrote down. Add up items 1, 4, 7, 9, and 10 to get your score on self-focused consistency.

Total self-focused consistency _____

Add up items 2, 3, 5, 6, and 8 to get your score on group-focused consistency.

Total group-focused consistency _____

Interpreting Your Self-Knowledge Scores

To determine what your numerical scores mean and where you fit into a general classification scheme consider the following guidelines for all three self-motives:

If you scored below 12.5 on the self-focus scale, you can consider yourself to be *low on that motive.*

If you scored above 17.5 on the group-focus scale, you can consider yourself to be *high on that motive.*

If you scored between 12.5 and 17.5 on the self- or group-focus scale, you are on the border and you may have both types of tendencies.

In the space provided below, place an "X" or check in the box that characterizes your self- or group-focus for the three self motives.

Place an "X" for your profile:

	Low Level	High Level	Borderline
Self-Enhancement			
Self-focus	_____	_____	_____
Group-focus	_____	_____	_____
Self-Growth			
Self-focus	_____	_____	_____
Group-focus	_____	_____	_____
Self-Consistency			
Self-focus	_____	_____	_____
Group-focus	_____	_____	_____
Total			
Self-focus	_____	_____	_____
Group-focus	_____	_____	_____

Now you can calculate your total score on the self- versus group focus motive across all three types of motives.

Self-focus: Add up all your three scores on self focus-enhancement, growth and consistency.

Total _____

Group-focus: Add up all your three scores on group-focus-enhancement, growth and consistency

Total _____

If your total score is lower than 37.5, on self-focus scale or the group-focus scale you can consider yourself to be low on the self-focus or group-focus motives.

If your total score is higher than 52.5, you can consider yourself to be high on self-focus or group-focus motives.

If your total score is between 37.5 and 52.5, you are on the border-line, and you may have both types of tendencies.

Next look at your cultural values score, and turn to Figure 3.2 and see what your profile is like. Compare it with the profiles of people who work for you. How do they compare? Are these motives and cultural orientations consistent with the type of management style that you use?

NOTES

Chapter 1

1. M. Erez and P. C. Earley, *Culture, Self-Identity, and Work* (Oxford: Oxford University Press, 1993).
2. "Inside GM's War Room," *Time*, December 13, 1993, 70.
3. M. Erez and P. C. Earley, *Culture, Self-Identity, and Work*.
4. Personal interview conducted by first author, 1991.

Chapter 2

1. M. Erez, and P. C. Earley, *Culture, Self-Identity, and Work* (Oxford: Oxford University Press, 1993).
2. V. Gecas, "The Self-Concept," *Annual Review of Psychology* 8 (1982): 1–33.
3. A. Bandura, *Social Foundations of Thoughts and Action: A Social Cognitive Theory* (Englewood Cliffs, N.J. Prentice-Hall, 1986).
4. J. A. Wall Jr., "Managers in the People's Republic of China," *Academy of Management Executive* 4 (1990): 25.
5. G. B. Northcraft, T. L. Griffith, and C. E. Shalley, "Building Top Management Muscle in a Slow Growth Environment: How Different is Better at Greyhound Financial Corporation," *Academy of Management Executive* 6 (1992): 35.
6. D. Eden, "Pygmalion, Goal-Setting, and Expectancy: Compatible Ways to Boost Productivity," *Academy of Management Review* 13 (1988) : 639–52.
7. V. Gecas, "The Self-Concept."
8. H. C. Triandis, "The Self and Social Behavior: Differing Cultural Contexts," *Psychological Review* 96 (1989): 506–20.

9. John Steinbeck, *America and Americans* (New York: Viking Press, 1966).
10. E. H. Schein, *Organizational Culture and Leadership* (San Francisco: Josey-Bass, 1985).
11. R. T. Pascale, and A. G. Athos, *The Art of Japanese Management* (New York: Simon & Schuster, 1981).
12. H. A. Witkin, 'and J. W. Berry, "Psychological Differentiation in Cross-Cultural Perspective," *Journal of Cross-Cultural Psychology* 6(1975):4–87.
13. A. Etzioni, *The Active Society* (New York: Free Press, 1968).
14. M. Mead, *Cooperation and Competition Among Primitive Peoples* (Boston: Beacon 1967).
15. G. Hofstede, *Culture and Organizations: Software of the Mind* (London: McGraw-Hill, 1991).

Chapter 3

1. R. J. House, W. D Spangler, and J. Woycke, "Personality and charisma in the U.S. Presidency: A Psychological Theory of Leader Effectiveness," *Administrative Science Quarterly* 36(1991): 364–96.
2. P. C. Earley, "Supervisors and Shop Stewards as Sources of Contextual Information in Goal-Setting: A Comparison of the U.S. with England," *Journal of Applied Psychology* 71 (1986): 111–18.
3. T. Matsui, T. Kakuyama, and M. L. Onglatco, "Effects of goals and feedback on performance in groups," *Journal of Applied Psychology* 72(1987): 407–15.
4. J. R. Hackman and G. R. Oldham, *Work Redesign* (Reading, Mass: Addison-Wesley, 1980).

Chapter 4

1. M. Erez and P. C. Earley, *Culture, Self-Identity, and Work* (Oxford: Oxford University Press, 1993).
2. M. S. Schall, "A Communication-Rules Approach to Organizational Culture" *Administrative Science Quarterly* 28(1983): 557–81.
3. S. Walton, *Sam Walton: Made in America — My Story* (New York: Bantam Books, 1992).
4. M. Erez and P. C. Earley, *Culture, Self-Identity, and Work.*
5. E. T. Hall, *Beyond Culture* (Garden City, New York: Doubleday 1976).
6. S. Ting-Toomey, "Toward a theory of conflict and culture," in W. Gudykunst, L. Stewart, and S. Ting-Toomey, eds., *Communication, Culture and Organizational Processes* (Beverly Hills, Calif.: Sage, 1985), 71–86.
7. M. Erez, "Interpersonal Communication Systems in Organizations, and their Relationships to Cultural Values, Productivity and Innovation: The Case of Japanese Corporations," *International Journal of Applied Psychology* 41(1992): 45–64.

8.   M. Erez, "Interpersonal Communication Systems.

9.   I. Nonaka, "Toward Middle-Up-Down Management: Accelerating Information Creation," *Sloan Management Review* Spring (1988): 9–18; U. Neisser, *Cognition and Reality: Principles and Implications of Cognitive Psychology* (San Francisco: W.H. Freeman and Company, 1976).

10. P. F. Druker, "What We Can Learn From Japanese Management," *Harvard Business Review* 49(1971): 110–22.

11. P. C. Earley, C. B. Gibson, and C. C. Chen, "How Did I Do Versus How Did We Do? Cultural Contrasts of Performance Feedback Search and Self-Efficacy," Unpublished paper, University of California, Irvine, 1995.

12. P. C. Earley, C. B. Gibson and C. C. Chen, "How Did I Do?"

13. Personal communication, 1994.

Chapter 5

1.   A. B. Fisher, "Morale Crisis," *Fortune,* November 18, 1991, 34–42.

2.   *Business Week,* May 1991, 52–76.

3.   *Business Week,* April 26, 1993, 38–39.

4.   K. Leung, and M. Bond, "The Impact of Cultural Collectivism on Reward Allocation," *Journal of Personality and Social Psychology* 47(1984): 793–804.

5.   K. Leung, and H. J. Park, "Effects of Interactional Goals on Choice of Allocation Rule: A Cross National Study," *Organizational Behavior & Human Decision Processes* 37(1986): 111–20.

6.   H. Thierry, "Payment by Results Systems: A Review of Research, 1945–1985," *Applied Psychology: An International Review* 36(1987): 91–108.

7.   *Business Week,* December 17, 1990, 44.

8.   J. L. Barsoux, and P. Lawrence, "The making of a French manager," *Harvard Business Review,* July–August (1991): 58–67.

9.   P. C. Earley, "Supervisor and shop stewards as sources of contextual information in goal-setting: A comparison of the U.S. with England," *Journal of Applied Psychology* 71(1986): 111–18.

10. M. Erez, and P. C. Earley, "Comparative Analysis of Goal-Setting Strategies Across Cultures," *Journal of Applied Psychology* 71(1987): 591–97.

11. M. Erez, "The Congruence of Goal-Setting Strategies with Socio-Cultural Values and its Effect on Performance," *Journal of Management* 12(1986): 83–90.

12. *Fortune,* June 1, 1992, 133.

13. R. Hackman, and G. Oldham, *Work Redesign* (Reading, Mass.: Addison-Wesley, 1980).

14. A. T. Stewart "Reengineering: The Hot New Managing Tool," *Fortune,* August 23, 1993, 33–37.

15. C. Berggren, "Nummi vs Uddevalla," *Sloan Management Review* Winter (1994): 37–49.
16. S. Prokesch, "Edges fray on Volvo's Brave New Humanistic World," *New York Times,* July 7, 1991, Business Section.
17. J. Byrne, "Horizontal Corporation: It's About Managing Across, Not Up and Down," *Business Week,* December 20, 1993, 76.

Chapter 6

1. E. E. Lawler III, *High Involvement Management* (San Francisco: Jossey-Bass, 1986).
2. "Clearly, the Team of the Decade," *Time,* January 8, 1990, 54
3. J. E. McGrath, *Groups: Interaction and Performance* (New Jersey: Prentice Hall, 1984).
4. M. Erez and P. C. Earley, *Culture, Self-Identity, and Work* (Oxford: Oxford University Press, 1993).
5. J. C. Turner, *Rediscovering the Social Group* (Oxford: Basil Blackwell, 1987).
6. D. Katz, and R. L. Kahn, *The Social Psychology of Organizations,* 2nd ed. (New York: Wiley, 1978).
7. E. A. Locke and G. P. Latham, *A Theory of Goal Setting and Task Performance* (Englewood Cliffs, NJ : Prentice-Hall, 1990).
8. J. R. Hackman, "Introduction," in J. R. Hackman, ed., *Groups that Work (and Those That Don't)* (San Francisco: Jossey-Bass, 1990).
9. E. A. Lind and T. R. Tyler, *The Social Psychology of Procedural Justice* (New York: Plenum, 1988).
10. J. O. Whittaker, and R. D. Meade, "Social Pressure in the Modification and Distortion of Judgment: A cross-cultural study," *International Journal of Psychology* 2 (1967): 109–13.
11. T. Matsui, T. Kakuyama, and M. L. Onglatco, "Effects of goals and feedback on performance in groups," *Journal of Applied Psychology* 72(1987): 407–15.

Chapter 7

1. N. Tichy and R. Chasan, "Speed, Simplicity and Self-Confidence: An Interview with Jack Welch," *Harvard Business Review* 67(1989): 112–21.
2. J. M. Burns, *Leadership* (New York: Harper and Row, 1978).
3. Personal conversation with House (May, 1990).
4. A. Zaleznik, "Managers and Leaders: Are They Different?" *Harvard Business Review* 55(5) (1977): 67–78.
5. R. G. Lord, "Functional leadership behavior: Measurement and Relation to Social Power and Leadership Perceptions," *Administrative Science Quarterly* 22(1977): 114–133.

6. M. Erez and P. C. Earley, *Culture, Self-Identity, and Work* (Oxford: Oxford University Press, 1993).
7. S. A. Kirkpatrick and E. A. Locke,"Leadership: Do Traits Matter?" *Academy of Management Executive* 5 (1991): 48–60.
8. R. Stogdill, *Handbook of Leadership: A Survey of the Literature* (New York: Free Press, 1974), 81.
9. J. A. Conger, "Theoretical foundations of charismatic leadership," in J. A. Conger and R. N. Kanungo, eds., *Charismatic Leadership* (San Francisco: Jossey-Bass, 1988).
10. M. F. R. Kets de Vries, "Origins of Charisma: Ties That Bind the Leader to the Led," In J. A. Conger and R. N. Kanungo, eds., *Charismatic Leadership* (San Francisco: Jossey-Bass, 1988).
11. S. E. Jackson, S. Zedeck, and E. Summers, "Family Life Disruptions: Effects of Induced Structual and Emotional Interference," *Academy of Management Journal* 28(1985): 574–86.
12. M. F. R. Kets de Vries, "Origins of Charisma."
13. S. A. Kirkpatrick and E. A. Locke,"Leadership."

Chapter 8

1. W. E. Deming, *Out of the Crisis* (Cambridge: Cambridge University Press, 1986).
2. B. Rather, *ISO-9000* (Aldershot, England: Gower, 1991).
3. K. Odaka, *Japanese management: A Forward Looking Analysis* (Tokyo: Japan Productivity Organization, 1986).
4. E. E. Lawler III, S. A. Mohrman, and G. E. Ledford Jr., *Employee Involvement and Total Quality Management: Practices and results in Fortune 1000 companies* (San Francisco: Jossey-Bass, 1992).
5. H. Robbers, and B. Sergeketter, *Quality is Personal: A Foundation for Total Quality Management* (New York: The Free Press, 1993).
6. R. Blackburn and B. Rosen, "Total Quality and HRM: Lessons Learned From the Baldridge Award-Winning Companies," *Academy of Management Executive* 7(1993): 49–67.
7. H. Sims and P. Lorenzi, *The New Leadership Paradigm* (Newbury Park, CA: Sage, 1992).
8. D. E. Bowen, and E. E. Lawler III, "Total Quality-Oriented Human Resources Management," *Organizational Dynamics* 10(1992): 29–41.
9. D. Kearns, "Leadership Through Quality," *Academy of Management Executive* 4 (1990): 86–89.
10. J. Brooke, "A New Quality in Brazil's Exports," *New York Times,* October 14, 1994, sec. d.
11. W. H. Miller, "Textbook Turnaround," *Industry Week* 20 (1992): 11–14.

12. "The Sputtering Spark from South America's Car Industry," *The Economist,* April 15, 1995, 57–58.
13. S. Baker, "If You Are Lucky, Your Next Car Will Be Made in Mexico," *Business Week,* Oct. 25, 1991,72.
14. M. H. Peak, "Maquiladoras: Where Quality is a Way of Life," *Management Review* (March 1993): 19–23.

Chapter 9

1. M. B. Teagarden, M. C. Butler, and M. A. Von Glinow, "Mexico's Maquiladora Industry: Where Strategic Human Resource Management Makes a Difference," *Organizational Dynamics* 20 (1992): 34–47.
2. E. A. Locke and G. P. Latham, *A Theory of Goal Setting and Task Performance* (Englewood Cliffs, NJ: Prentice-Hall, 1990).
3. D. Katz, and R. L. Kahn, *The Social Psychology of Organizations,* 2nd ed. (New York: Wiley, 1978).

SUGGESTED READINGS

General Country Specific Information
Baedekker's Guides
Country Chambers of Commerce
Foreign Embassies and Travel Bureaus
Local Country Interest Groups
Microsoft Encarta

Business Information

Adler, N. J. *International Dimensions of Organizational Behavior.* 2nd ed. Boston: PWS-Kent, 1991.

Bond, M. *Beyond the Chinese Face.* Hong Kong: Oxford University Press, 1988.

Brockner, J. *Self-Esteem at Work: Research, Theory, and Practice.* Lexington, Mass. Lexington Books, 1988.

Dowling, P. J., and R. S. Schuler, *International Dimensions of Human Resource Management.* Boston: PWS-Kent, 1990 .

Earley, P. C., and M. Erez, *New Perspectives on International Industrial/ Organizational Psychology.* San Francisco: Jossey-Bass Publishers. In press .

England, G. W. *The Manager and His Values: An International Perspective from the United States, Japan, Korea, India, and Australia.* Cambridge, Mass: Ballinger Press, 1975.

Erez, M., and P. C. Earley, *Culture, Self-Identity, and Work.* New York: Oxford University Press, 1993.

Gannon, M. J. *Understanding Global Cultures: Metaphorical Journeys Through Seventeen Countries.* Newbury Park, Calif.: Sage, 1994.

Graham, J. L., and Y. Sano, *Smart Bargaining: Doing Business With the Japanese.* Los Angeles: Sano Management Corporation, 1989.

Gyllenhammer, P. G., How Volvo Adapts Work to People. *Harvard Business Review* 55(1977): 102–113.

Hampden-Turner, C., and A. Trompenaars, *The Seven Cultures of Capitalism: Value Systems for Creating Wealth in the United States, Japan, Germany, France, Britain, Sweden, and the Netherlands.* New York: Currency Doubleday, 1993.

Harris, P. R., and R. T. Moran, *Managing Cultural Differences.* Houston, Tex.: Gulf, 1979.

Hofstede, G. *Culture's consequences: International Differences in Work-related Values.* Beverly Hills, Calif.: Sage Publications, 1980.

Hofstede, G. *Culture and Organizations: Software of the Mind.* London: McGraw-Hill, 1991.

Martin, J. *Cultures in Organizations: Three Perspectives.* New York: Oxford University Press, 1993.

Mitsubishi Corporation. *Tatemae and Honne: Distinguishing Between Good Form and Real Intention in Japanese Business Culture.* New York: Free Press, 1988.

Moran, R. T., and P. R. Harris, *Managing Cultural Synergy.* Houston, Tex.: Gulf, 1981.

Porter, M. E. *The Competitive Advantage of Nations.* New York: Free Press, 1990.

Schein, E. *Organizational Culture and Leadership.* San Francisco: Jossey-Bass, 1985.

Ting-Toomey, S., and F. Korzenny, *Cross-Cultural Interpersonal Communication.* Newbury Park, Calif.: Sage, 1991.

Triandis, H. C. *Culture and Social Behavior.* New York: McGraw-Hill, 1994.

Triandis, H. C., M. D. Dunnette, and L. M. Hough, *Handbook of Industrial and Organizational Psychology.* Vol. 4, Palo Alto, Calif.: Consulting Psychologists Press, 1994.

Whyte, D. *The Heart Aroused: Poetry and the Preservation of the Soul in Corporate America.* New York: Currency Doubleday, 1994.

Yip, G. S. *Total Global Strategy: Managing for Worldwide Competitive Advantage.* Englewood Cliffs, N J: Prentice Hall, 1992.

Ziera, Y. Management Development in Ethnocentric Multinational Corporations. *California Management Review,* 18(1976): 34–42.

Index